CHILD of the
SOUTH DAKOTA
FRONTIER

CHILD of the SOUTH DAKOTA FRONTIER

Based on the Writing of Lenna Kolash

BROWN BOOKS
PUBLISHING GROUP

Child of the South Dakota Frontier

Brown Books Publishing Group
16250 Knoll Trail Drive, Suite 205
Dallas, Texas 75248
www.BrownBooks.com
(972) 381-0009

A New Era in Publishing™

ISBN 978-1-61254-156-3
LCCN 2014931258

Printed in the United States
10 9 8 7 6 5 4 3 2 1

For more information or to contact the author, please go to
www.SouthDakotaFrontier.com

Dedication

Lenna Kolash, you were a wife, a teacher, a writer, and, most of all, a loving mother who always had the best interests of her daughters' lives in her heart throughout her own life. Here's to you, Mom, a daughter's gift of the publication of your beloved book, *Child of the South Dakota Frontier.*

Contents

Acknowledgments

John Farmer, husband of thirty years, thank you for your generous support of time and financial caring for publishing Mom's book. Thanks to my dad, William Kolash, who is now deceased but was very encouraging to me to see this book published. Susan McCarrol, my sister, thank you for searching for the wonderful pictures that appear in the book. Finally thanks to Karen Umlauf, Mom's student teacher in the late 1960s. She and my mom had a wonderful relationship, and Karen and I have kept in touch through many years. She has given me strength and support to keep on "truck'n down that lonely road" of publishing rejections finally to see our work come to fruition. Karen also came up with the title *Child of the South Dakota Frontier.*

1956

Chapter 1

The Tree

(left to right) Betty Jo, Bill,
Lenna, and Susan Kolash

A dry wind swept over eroded draws and treeless hills dotted with sagebrush. Fine, white dust tortured the dying grass along the shoulders of the black macadam that wound down from the Black Hills of South Dakota and cut a straight line across my childhood home lying prostrate under the withering sun.

My husband, Bill, and I sat in the front seat of our station wagon, looking out at the brick ranch houses on the outskirts of Edgemont. The girls sat in the back, by turns whispering and fussing at each other, oblivious to the dusty ranch town. One of them did notice the sickly green waste that stained the Cheyenne River bank behind the uranium mill: "Yuck."

I didn't mind. Main Street turned back into a two-lane blacktop, and we headed further south across the flat plains. My eyes feasted on the gray sagebrush and the folds of sterile shale in the gullies, where, as a child, I'd found fossils hidden in the crevices. I recalled the intense red and gold sunsets that lit my way as my horse and I drove the milk cows home. For me, the barren, parched ground and the burning, white summer skies held treasures I'd hoarded for years.

These were my memories, not the scary times, when I'd been asked to shoulder more than I thought I could bear, and not the hardships my father and mother did bear to the point of breaking. They'd traveled west to do mission work, sent by The Home Mission in Pierre. My father had come from Ireland seven years earlier to study for the ministry in Chicago. He'd met my mother there, and after they married, they'd served several churches before answering the call in 1913 to preach in Edgemont.

Then, as now, the spruce-dotted Black Hills to the north towered over the red bluffs carved by the broad, snaking

Cheyenne River. The Lakota Sioux had already been confined to two nearby reservations—the Pine Ridge in the foothills and the Rosebud along the Nebraska line.

Over the nearly fifty years since I'd lived in Edgemont, the town had thrived and then declined. It wasn't much more than a depot along the rail line in 1890, but once the government opened the prairies south and west of town to homesteaders, it grew quickly. By the time we arrived, most of the land fit to be farmed had claims filed on them, and the homesteaders had cut up the range south of town with their barbed wire fences.

The Edgemont of my childhood bustled with home-steaders coming in for their supplies. The cattle and sheep men used the town too and shipped their cattle out by rail. Only one family had an automobile. The streets were crowded with wagons and buggies kicking up swirls of dust. A few homes had electricity, but many houses were still lit with kerosene lamps. Telephone lines were just beginning to thread out onto the plains. Indians, down from the Pine Ridge, clutched their blankets around their store clothes and slipped along on moccasined feet, stopping to stare into the windows of the strange, new houses.

That was the town my parents brought us to. They'd chosen to do their part in taming the Wild West, but they could not have predicted that my father would be forced to abandon his ministry and turn to farming a corner of the earth that resisted his efforts with one natural or unnatural disaster after another. Only the strongest endured in that hard country. My father was not among them.

Our station wagon climbed to the crest of a low hill, and a cluster of gray buildings appeared in the distance, scattered beside a railroad track like a tumbled tower of wooden blocks. "Provo!" I cried.

One of the girls muttered, "That's a town?"

Yes. A town. My Provo, where I had been battered by hail, drenched in rain, whipped by blizzards, and blistered by sun. But I had also known this land when the water holes were full, and gentle showers washed purple flowers into the thawed plains. I had seen the cactus crowned by mounds of waxy yellow bloom. Plumes of fragrant lavender shot from silver sagebrush. I had played with colts and calves and lambs beneath warm skies and ridden my horse bareback and carefree in the cool dusk. My daughters saw none of this, of course. Only the sad remnants of my prairie childhood.

I'd suggested this afternoon drive to show my family where I'd spent the happiest and hardest years of my childhood. So far, they were unimpressed. I told Bill to stop at a weathered, white bungalow with an oasis of manicured lawn. A swinging sign over the driveway read, "America's Finest Lambs, Ed Sykes."

A brown dog trotted up to me, panting in the heat, eyeing me. He followed me up the steps and sniffed me as I knocked on the door. I shivered a little, though a breath of hot breeze swept across the back of my neck.

At last the door opened. "Yes?" A middle-aged, wind-worn man stared at me with clear, blue eyes slitted against the sunlight.

"You don't remember me, Eddie," I blurted. "I'm Lenna O'Neill!"

"Well, I'll be darned!"

He drew me into the coolness of the darkened house. "Betty, come quick. Here's an old friend."

"I was afraid you weren't here when I saw the blinds down."

"Trying to keep the heat out. Been pretty hot all summer."

"It usually is, isn't it? At least that's the way I remember it."

I laughed and he did too. Then we lapsed into an awkward silence. I felt a rush of shyness until Betty broke in, asking if I'd like to call in the family.

"Thank you, no. We don't have much time. I really want to show them the old place, but everything looks so different. I don't think I can find it."

"Nothing left there for you to see," Ed said.

"Not anything?"

"I tore everything down when I bought the place. Sold the tile from your big house to an outfit building up by Piedmont."

"Could you show us the way out there?"

He clapped on a straw hat, and we went out into the blazing afternoon. Eddie sat in front with Bill and navigated. "Turn left at the railroad track. We'll go down the valley road and up through the pasture. Recognize the old schoolhouse?" he asked me, gesturing toward a dilapidated structure I remembered as newly built. Several boarded storefronts had "Closed" hand painted across the doors.

"Nothing much left here since the government closed the munitions depot," said Eddie pointing to distant acres of rusting metal domes.

We turned down the valley road. A long string of rusty, graffiti-covered boxcars rumbled along beside us. I remembered the huge, gleaming steam engines that used to whistle at Hopper's Crossing and roar down our valley, scattering cinders that sparked little prairie fires.

"Whoa," Eddie exclaimed. "Here we are."

Bill turned onto a grass-choked lane, and Eddie got out to open the wood gate. The shriveled remains of a jackrabbit hung from the wire fence by the post.

Eddie pointed out the barely discernible trail that led through the dry grass of our bottomland and up the slow rise.

"Be careful of the cactus and greasewood. No tire's a match for them."

Bill's arms wound around the steering wheel, jerking from side to side as he maneuvered up the rutted lane. At the top of the hill, my eyes scanned the flatland that stretched all the way to the Black Hills in the distance.

"Where is everyone?" I cried. "There's hardly a house or building left."

"Ma and Pa are long gone. Sally lives down near the Nebraska line. Harry lives in Casper. Jim was lost in World War II."

The losses—his and mine—weighed on my heart. My home and the friends that had populated it had all but disappeared, and my initial excitement at the prospect of sharing my past with my girls dampened to a bittersweetness that caught in my throat. "What happened to all the wheat that used to grow here? And where are the cattle?"

"Nothing much but sheep in the valley now. I run a few here on your old place."

Sheep! Unbelievable, I thought.

A chain of boxcars rumbled across the top of an earthen mound less than a quarter of a mile away, above the pond where my sister and I had learned to swim by watching how the frogs did it. Now the stagnant water looked too shallow and rank for kids or frogs.

"Remember when our fathers built that dam together?"

"Ah, yes." My throat ached with the remembering.

"OK, Bill. You can stop here," Ed said.

I stepped out of the car and onto the ground my parents and I had walked, shielding my eyes from the harsh sunlight. The spare, stiff prairie grass crackled beneath my feet and prickled my ankles. Masses of pale green cactus with thorny heads and gnarled gray clumps of sagebrush wandered over the cracked, hard earth. My heart cried out in protest.

"Here's where the big house stood," Ed said. He pointed to a shallow dip in the land and kicked a rusty stove leg from the hardpan. "The old house and the barns were over there."

I tried looking east to orient myself, but all I saw was more overgrazed prairie. Where I expected to see Dad Jahns' place, a clump of trees huddled like cattle in a storm. I asked Ed if that was the old orchard.

"Those are seedling cottonwoods around the water hole."

Glory be! Wouldn't Father have been delighted to know that, contrary to Dad Jahns' dire predictions, the still hadn't spoiled the water hole.

Despair swept over me when I surveyed our hard-won garden reclaimed by cactus. The house my father built with his own hands had been dismantled and hauled away. The dreams of my mother's life had scattered in harsh winter winds and hot summer breezes. My home, the prairie, and all that I had loved had disappeared like a mirage.

I was heading back to the car when I saw the little cedar my father and I had planted by the garden gate. Still dwarfed, it nevertheless stood green and erect, almost obscured by crowding sagebrush. It hadn't grown much in forty years, but miraculously, it had survived. I rubbed its soft needles and inhaled the sharp, familiar aroma. Voices of the past echoed. Memories rolled away the years, and I was home again, a child of the South Dakota frontier.

1913

Chapter 2

We Arrive

Thick snow fell in the cold night air. The train hissed. A few men worked rapidly alongside the rail cars, dimly outlined by the swinging glow of their lanterns. Except for the trainmen, we were alone in the gray night.

"Mrs. O'Neill?" We turned to see a wiry, little man in a black bowler hat approaching through the snow. "Welcome to Edgemont, ma'am."

"You must be Mr. Blackney," Mother said.

"Sorry to give you such a cold reception, but March weather is always the worst, it seems," he said raising his hat.

"How do you do," Mother said.

Mr. Blackney shook hands with Verna and me just as if we were grownups. "Are you young ladies twins?"

Being the shy one, I couldn't find my voice with the stranger.

"No," Verna said. "Lenna's five and I'm four."

He turned back to Mother, keeping hold of our hands. "It's just a short way to our place, and the missus is waiting supper."

Since we'd arrived, the platform had filled with rail workers, jostling, shouting, hurrying to get on the train. Others streamed past us and disappeared into the night. "Crews change here,"

Mr. Blackney explained. He steered us through the throng to a snow-covered wooden sidewalk and up a dimly lit street. The deepening snow muffled our footsteps, and an eerie stillness descended. Verna and I held tight to each other's hands.

"I understand the Reverend arrives tomorrow."

"Yes, he's coming on the freight with our furniture and our dog, Queen." I knew Father had saved paying a fare by riding in the freight car, but Mother didn't tell that part to Mr. Blackney.

"As soon as he arrives, we'll get you folks moved into the parsonage, but tonight, you stay with us." We paused in front of a jewelry store. I noticed a fine display of gold and silver pocket watches resting on velvet stands. "This is our store. We live upstairs," he said, leading us through the darkened space.

A round, gray-haired woman in a white apron smiled at us from the top of the stairs. A wave of loneliness swept over me at the sight of her. She reminded me of Grandmother, whom we had left behind in Ree Heights. The aroma of roast chicken and biscuits quickly dispelled the sadness, and the warmth of the potbellied stove soothed our train-weary bodies.

In our bedroom, Mother tipped the big white pitcher for water to wash our soot-covered hands, and before she let us go to supper she smoothed our braids and retied our hair ribbons. All the years we lived on the frontier, Mother never let us forget that we were well-trained young ladies. She'd come to Edgemont carrying the Word and a civilized sensibility, and she wasn't about to let us succumb to the wildness of the West.

To our delight, Verna and I found polished silver cups next to our plates. "They're just a little welcome gift," Mr. Blackney said. I felt my heart warm. We smiled for the first time that night and thanked him. Edgemont might not be so bad after all, I thought.

"We're sorely in need of the influence of an active church," Mr. Blackney said after grace. "Railroad towns are notorious. Train crews lay over at the end of their runs, and they have too much time for gambling and the like."

Mother paled a bit. "Oh, don't worry," he said. We have some fine solid church people here too, don't we Effie?"

"The noise from all the trains will bother you for awhile," Mrs. Blackney said.

I had a hard time paying attention to the conversation between bites of buttery biscuits, fluffy as little clouds and chicken with crispy skin and juice that flowed when I cut into it.

"We knew it wouldn't be easy when we accepted the call," Mother said in her soft, quiet voice, not her preaching voice.

"You'll get used to the trains," Mrs. Blackney said, waving her hand. "The Burlington roars through twice a day on its way to Helena, Montana, or back to Omaha. That whistle screams and the brakes screech when it rolls in, and then those engineers think they have to pull the whistle again on the way out. I declare, I'd like to tell them a thing or two."

"My husband is a light sleeper, but we'll get used to it, I'm sure," Mother said.

"Now, don't you worry about it," Mr. Blackney said. He glanced at his wife. "Isn't that right?"

She nodded in agreement and handed Mother the platter of chicken.

"Westerners are the friendliest, best-hearted folks you'll ever find," he said. "Life isn't easy here, but we're great next-year people. Nothing ever licks us."

Mrs. Blackney poured more coffee. "One of our toughest challenges is getting enough water. We have to buy it off the tank wagon. It comes around twice a week."

Mother's eyes widened. "Don't you have a well or river water?" I watched her cheeks color just like they did on the train when the waiter said they didn't have milk for Verna and me. "The map showed the Cheyenne flowing very near this town."

"Hah!" Mrs. Blackney rolled her eyes to the ceiling. "The only time the Cheyenne really flows is in spring or after a cloudburst in summer. Most of the time it's nothing but mud, and during dry spells, it's downright dusty."

Mother was getting unnerved. Her voice rose. "So where does the water you buy come from?"

"Ed Sykes pumps it from a spring across the valley near the foot of Gull Hill and delivers it on his wagon," Mr. Blackney said. "Some folks buy it from the railroad. They bring tank cars in from somewhere in the Black Hills with water for the trains. It's five cents a bucket."

He tried to make it sound like it wasn't a big problem, but Mrs. Blackney had a different perspective. "I'll tell you what, water is the biggest challenge a woman faces in this town. There's a rain barrel by the parsonage back door, but that water's for dishwashing and bathing and isn't too handy when it's frozen in the winter anyway."

"Now, Effie, you mustn't paint the picture so dark." I thought for a minute Mr. Blackney was going to pat Mother's hand, but his finger tapped the table instead. "We're drilling a new well. We've tried in the past, but even when we dug deep, the water was thick with minerals. The cattle wouldn't even drink it."

A slow shake of her head told me Mother didn't like that news one bit.

"Don't you worry. There's hope," Mr. Blackney said. "The railroad is helping us out with this new well. We're already down more than 2,000 feet. We struck alkali water a couple times, so we had to seal that off and go deeper. We'll find good water yet."

Mrs. Blackney asked us if we wanted some vanilla pudding, one of my favorites, but I couldn't answer for yawning. Mother taught us to always put our hands in front of our mouths, but I remembered too late.

To my relief, she overlooked the transgression. "I'm afraid the girls are pretty tired. If you'll excuse us, I'll hear their prayers and tuck them in."

"You girls sleep well," Mrs. Blackney said. "Before you know it, that Queen dog and your papa will be here."

On the soft mattress and under a deep pile of quilts, I drifted toward sleep, but not before I asked God to keep Papa and Queen safe in the boxcar rolling west to our new home.

Chapter 3

The Well

I woke up to Mother standing by the bed in her nightgown, the kerosene lamp held high in her hand.

"Get up, girls! Get up! Hurry, get dressed!"

I squeezed my eyes shut against the yellow light. The church bell clanged and the roundhouse whistle shrilled. Footsteps clattered on the wooden sidewalk in front of our house and the hooves of galloping horses pounded the unpaved street. I knew that only a catastrophe could raise such a commotion in the dark of night.

Mother helped me with buttons and stockings, her trembling hands flying from one to the other. One of my braids caught on a button, but I was too frightened to complain. Verna, still half asleep, cried and threw herself back onto the bed.

Father appeared in the doorway. "No crying now! Get up! Get up!" At his excited tone, Verna scrambled out of bed. "Help Mama get you dressed. I'm going outside to see what I can find out."

My father shouted out the front door to someone passing by. "My goodness, man! What has happened?"

"The well's come in! It's a gusher!"

The huge relief didn't dampen our excitement. We hurried to join the throng. Though we hadn't been in Edgemont long, we'd already come to know what a well would mean to every family.

The church bell rang so loud it vibrated Mother's dishes in the cupboard. Mother threw her blue dress on over her nightgown. Her long dark brown hair coiled loosely under her black hat. I'd never seen her step outside the house without being perfectly put together. She slipped into the coat Father held for her and said, "Girls, put on your angora hoods. You don't want to get an earache." Even in the heat of this moment, she couldn't stop worrying over us.

The moon hung bright and high in the cloudless sky. Our breaths puffed like smoke, preceding us as we hurried to join the others. We were met by an enormous cloud of vapor roiling into the air. It rose higher than the church steeple, rushing toward the stars, dimming the moonlight. The gushing water nearly drowned out every other sound. At the edge of the well, a heavy mist settled on all of our parched faces. The church bells and the roundhouse whistle kept on. I gripped Father's hand. I'd never been in such a boisterous crowd and certainly not in the middle of the night. Long shadows danced and dark figures loomed all around me. Even Mother and Father were taller than usual in my eyes.

We found Mr. Blackney standing there in long johns and boots under his big coat. "Isn't this wonderful?" he shouted, spreading his arms at the sight.

"Just look at all that water!" Father shouted.

"Let me see," I demanded, and Father lifted me to his shoulders.

At last I could see the water shooting into the night sky and then falling hard upon the dirt, rushing along the railroad embankment and past the platform into a depression, where it fed an ever-widening pool. A breeze kicked up and carried a spray of drops over the crowd, and we erupted in squeals and laughter.

Moments passed before I became aware of a stench so horrible it choked me. I squirmed, and Father set me down to be engulfed again by the tall, dark forms all around me. Someone yelled, "Must have gone clean to hell for it! Smells like sulphur and brimstone."

Mr. Bartlett, one of the town fathers, puffed out his rather large, round chest. "Bet you never saw anything like this in Ireland!"

Father shook his head in wonder. Mother leaned against Father, holding her coat closed tight around her. I hadn't seen her look so happy since we'd arrived in Edgemont. The lack of water bothered her, but more than that, she worried about Father's health. The noise of the town was particularly hard on him. The long trains shook the town with their rumbling and whistling. Settlers' wagons rattled over the dirt street in front of our house, and the hollering from the saloons robbed his peace at night, worsening his chronic insomnia. Verna and I grew accustomed to the darkened house, quiet much of the day while Father tried to sleep after tossing all night.

But this night was different. We were all awake with Father, joining in the big excitement. I couldn't have named it back then, at age five, but I recognized hope in my parents' smiling faces.

"Is the water hot, or is it because the night is so cold that it seems as though it's steaming?" Mother asked Mr. Bartlett.

"That's real hot water, ma'am," he said. "But so long as it's good water, we'll figure out what to do with it."

People gathered closer, and Mr. Bartlett's voice got even louder to accommodate his audience. "Drilled 2,980 feet. No wonder it's hot water. That smell means it's an artesian well. We've got plenty of those hereabouts. So long as it tastes all right, guess we can put up with the smell." The crowd murmured in agreement.

"At the rate it's coming out of the ground, it'll run dry before you get the damn thing capped," someone said.

"We've sent word to the Lusk oil field over in Wyoming. They'll send someone to cap it. Nobody here knows what to do with a gusher like this," Mr. Bartlett said.

After a while, we headed back home with high hopes. I took a last look at the steam rising above the dim lights of the town and wondered how anything that smelled that bad could be good.

The crew from Wyoming capped the well by the third day. Banking on success, a large reservoir had been constructed on the rise west of town when the well digging had begun. Some of the pipes had already been laid. With the water flowing at 675 gallons per minute, it didn't take long to fill the reservoir, but it was late summer before we could draw water at the parsonage. We washed dishes and took baths in it just as it came from the faucet. The hard water had to be "broken" with lye or water softener before it could be used for washing clothes, but that was no different than the water we'd been getting from Ed's truck.

The water stayed hot in the reservoir, so Mother cooled some of it in fruit jars for drinking. "Do you know what's the first thing hoboes ask me at the back door these days?" 'Lady, do you have a cold drink of water? I'm so thirsty for cold water.'"

That spring of 1913, all the talk centered on water, and for the first time in the history of Edgemont, the question wasn't how to get it but what to do with the new abundance. Folks considered piping it directly from the well to heat their houses.

The town fathers floated a plan to pipe in the mineral water and create a sanitarium.

"For goodness sake," said Mother. "The vile odor from that water is enough to kill or cure anything. But wherever did they get the idea that water has medicinal qualities?"

Chapter 4

The Trip to Provo

Dora and Joseph O'Neill

The buggy bounced over the rutted road that led up Skene Hill along a narrow shelf. Mother sat on the outside. She kept her face turned toward the hill, refusing to look at the steep drop. Father had the reins, and he made a show of leaning back and relaxing to enjoy the view and the warm sunshine.

The higher we climbed, the harder Mother clutched the armrest. "Joe, how long are we—"

"Look there!" He broke in and pointed ahead, pulling back on the reins.

"Where? What? Oh, Joe, you're driving so near the edge of the road!" Mother cried.

Father slid the whip from its cup and pointed.

"Beside that rock. See the snake?"

We all leaned forward. I held my breath as my hard gaze followed the whip. A thick, earth-colored snake moved slowly and gracefully, then slipped over the embankment and disappeared. When we passed the spot, Father and Verna and I peered down, but the snake, camouflaged by sagebrush and shale, was nowhere to be found.

"That was a rattler. If ever you find yourself near one, just stand still and it will try to get away," Father said. "They don't attack unless provoked or frightened."

"We had a few back in Nebraska when I was a girl," Mother said, still looking straight ahead as if she could steer the buggy and avoid all dangers with the power of her eyes alone.

"Art Bartlett says this part of the country is infested with them," Father said. "Here I am, an Irishman spared of all snakes, and I end up in the Wild West, living in a snake pit."

Mother put her arm around his shoulder and smiled up at him. I knew she was thinking of how strange it was that we'd landed here. Father had come from Ireland only seven years earlier. His father had had considerable land, a large house, and servants to help with the work. The green hills near the lakes of Killarny were a far cry from the dry, golden grasslands of South Dakota. Father liked to tell us stories of his childhood. Crowding his memories were verdant fields, pest bogs, hedges, and rock walls with stiles for crossing, roses like cabbages, a glass-enclosed conservatory where exotic plants, grapes, peaches, and tomatoes were grown.

Father had come to the states to study for the ministry at the Moody Bible Institute in Chicago, where Mother was also training for the ministry. They met and married, and after graduation, they served small churches in Wisconsin and eastern South Dakota. The Home Mission Director in Pierre wrote to them about Edgemont, "a Wild West town but a growing frontier community with great opportunity for the work of the Lord."

The Home Mission pledged six hundred dollars a year, and the rest of the salary would come from church collections and gifts. At almost the same time, Father's doctor said to him, "Those delicate lungs you inherited from your Irish ancestors could be helped by dry western air, Reverend O'Neill." That settled it. Father and Mother accepted "the call."

Mother had grown up in eastern Nebraska, where life was gentler. She was unaccustomed to the uncultured life of the Wild West. But they'd promised to do the work of the Lord, and that turned out to be in Edgemont. Father had been asked to go to nearby Provo, another town without a preacher, to hold an afternoon service.

"It's a beautiful day for the trip," Father had said after we had eaten a hasty lunch at the parsonage. "Now, please be ready when I come back from the livery stable."

"Do you think its warm enough for me to wear my light coat?" Mother asked him.

"Yes. It's like summer," he said as he went out the door.

He returned driving two brown horses hitched to a shiny black, red-wheeled buggy with the top down.

"My, we're traveling in style," Mother exclaimed. "Verna, take this footstool out to Papa. Lenna, you carry the Irish robe." She picked up Father's brown satchel and followed us out to the buggy.

Verna sat between Mother and Father and I on the stool at their feet. We rode down the streets of Edgemont, up over the schoolhouse hill, down again over the Burlington tracks, and up Skene Hill.

Not long after we passed the snake, we arrived at the top of a mesa. The breeze that had been so balmy down in the valley blew cooler. Mother buttoned her coat at the neck. She pulled out the Irish robe and tucked it around us. The team trotted past several farms before it brought us to the hog-backs, a series of steep, rocky ridges that lifted us to rolling green prairies dotted with cactus and sagebrush. The air grew steadily cooler and the wind increased. I pulled the heavy plaid blanket closer about me and pushed the tickling fringe away from my face.

"Don't," cried Verna. "You've got me all untucked!"

"Now, girls, don't quarrel. Lenna, move back closer to Verna. Then you'll both be warmer. We must be almost there," Mother said, sounding rather unconvincing.

A downhill slope led us into Provo, which was nothing but a few buildings beside the railroad track. The little town was a flag stop on the Burlington route. Settlers who had established their claims nearby bought their supplies from the Provo General Store and received their mail from the post office set up at one end of the long counter. They had built a schoolhouse near the railroad station, which was also used for church services when they could get a preacher to come out.

Horses pulling lumber wagons, buggies, spring wagons, and a surrey stood all in a row at the hitching rails before the schoolhouse. A man and a boy stepped up to the buggy when we pulled up.

"Afternoon, Reverend," the man said. "You folks go on in. Eric and I will tie up your team."

"Thank you. I hope we aren't late," Father said. I knew he was just being polite. He'd been consulting his gold pocket watch all along the way. I was glad we were there at last for I was cold. Mother was so chilled and cramped she limped a little when she first got down.

Every seat in the schoolhouse was filled. The girls and women sat huddled together, two to rectangular benches set behind a narrow desk. The men and boys sat in extra chairs or stood at the back of the room. Friendly, curious looks greeted us, and the din of chatter quieted as we filed in. Father hung his coat on an iron hook and offered to take Mother's, but she shook her head. She tried to smile when he introduced her, but her teeth chattered so much that her face remained frozen. Some of the ladies offered us their seats by the stove, and we didn't hesitate to accept them. A short, red-faced man approached Mother carrying a folded fur robe.

"Name's Worthington, ma'am. Wrap up in this buffalo robe and you'll be warm in no time. The old lady and I always have it on the seat of the wagon. No telling when we'll need it around here. It makes sitting a little easier too."

Mother raised her hands in polite refusal, but he persisted.

"Try it, ma'am. You'll be surprised at how warm it is."

Mother finally relented and wrapped herself in it from head to foot, looking more like the native Indian women I'd seen in picture books than a refined preacher from Ree Heights. The wind continued to blow outside, but the crowd and the fragrant wood in the stove kept the room comfortably warm.

Father pulled his Bible, his songbook, and a sheaf of papers from his satchel and made his way to the small platform at the front of the room. He was wearing his best suit and his stiff, white collar, as he did whenever he left the house. Mother teased Father about the care with which he dressed before going out in public, but he insisted. "They have a right to expect their minister to look and act like a gentleman. How can I demand respect if I don't look as though I deserve it?"

Mother often said, while she waited impatiently for him to be ready to go someplace, "If the house were burning down, the man would come out the last minute with every button buttoned and his shoes shined."

We knew, of course, that she really was very proud of him and his gentility. His courtly, old-world manners; his immaculate clothes; his carefully trimmed mustache; his Irish brogue distinguished him.

He worked hard to prepare for his Sunday sermons. Most days, he went into his room, and we didn't see him till noon. We might hear him pacing up and down, opening bookcase doors, turning in the swivel chair before his desk, but we knew he was preparing the sermon and must not be disturbed.

Father arranged his materials on the teacher's desk and cleared his throat. The crowd hushed. "Shall we begin our service by singing hymn number 421?"

A plump young woman played the first notes on the organ. Everyone stood, causing more commotion. Mother rose from the folds of the buffalo robe and joined everyone in singing, "This is my story, this is my song, praising my Savior, all the day long."

Announcements and the passing of the collection plate followed Father's reading of the scripture and a prayer. Then he launched into his sermon, his strong, deep voice taking over the room. Since I'd already heard it in the morning service, my mind began to wander. I ran my fingers over the wood desktop and looked for pictures in the marks and cuts. I investigated the round metal lid set into the back ledge and discovered that the small glass container underneath lifted out. With blue ink on my fingers, I glanced at Mother and found her staring at me and shaking her head in disapproval. Her stern gaze encouraged me to redouble my efforts to concentrate on Father.

His blue eyes seemed to look straight at me as he spoke. Though he was quite thin and of average height, he appeared taller when he preached. With his wavy black hair, fine features, and pale complexion, dressed in a swallow-tailed pulpit coat, starched white collar and cuffs peeking out, he cut a dashing figure next to the ruddy-faced and roughly dressed men looking up at him, attending to his every word.

Verna, sitting across the aisle beside Mother, slept with her head resting on the desk. I laid my head down too, but unlike Verna, I couldn't sleep. She could close her eyes and doze off anywhere, but I was too curious at everything going on around me. With my cheek against the cool surface of the desk, I looked at the children sitting quietly beside their mothers or fidgeting to get down. A little girl with blue ribbons on braids crossed behind her ears stared at me just as intently as I stared at her. My gaze shifted to the front of the room where cutout-yellow paper ducks lined the top of the blackboard behind my father. A large octagonal clock hung on the wall next to the American flag. The loud ticking nearly sent me to sleep, and I no longer heard the words of the sermon.

My eyes drifted to Mother, who had thrown back the buffalo robe from her shoulders and slipped off her coat. In her blue dress, flushed from the warmth of the stove and the robe, she looked more beautiful than any other woman in the room. Though she'd already heard the sermon at morning service, she never took her large, dark brown eyes off Father. I felt proud of my parents and secure in the knowledge that our family had been embraced by this tiny community in the so-called Wild West.

Father raised the buggy hood, and we drew close under the Irish blanket, bracing ourselves for the long ride home.

"Hope you won't catch cold, Joe. Worries me for you to be in this cold air after the way you were perspiring during the sermon," Mother said. "Maybe I should have accepted the loan of that smelly, dusty buffalo robe, but I couldn't bear the thought of having it over me anymore." Mother worried constantly over Father's health. After two sermons and the long buggy ride, signs of fatigue lined his face.

He let the horses trot at a fast clip, and we moved steadily along the meandering ruts of the rough road. The wind died down a bit as the sun creeped lower in the sky. I watched Father's hands tighten on the reins as we rounded a bend. Leaning against his leg, I sensed his body growing tense. Then I saw why. Twenty or thirty horses emerged from a rocky coulee no more than a few yards ahead. The leader of the herd stopped short, ears forward, his attention on our horses and the rig. As the rest of the horses scrambled out of the ravine, they jostled each other, tossed their heads, snorted, and formed a united front trotting toward us.

Our team pressed on, their ears flicked, sensing danger. Father took the whip out of its stock. Our team trotted faster.

"Must be horses turned loose on the plains to forage for themselves. I imagine they'll be rounded up for spring work," Father said. First a chestnut, then a black sidled up to the buggy and trotted along with us. Others, several colts among them, fell in behind us. Soon, we were nearly surrounded.

Father held the team to a steady trot along the road. No one breathed a word. The range horses snorted, kicked, and squealed, shouldering each other and jockeying for position. They nipped and whinnied and chased each other away, then circled back to the buggy. My heart pounded. Father's leg jiggled with nerves. Mother's hand flew to her mouth.

Then, almost as quickly as they joined us, they drew back and streamed off at a gallop to the east. Only then did Father call attention to the coyote at the edge of the herd.

"That's no coyote," Mother cried, "That's a wolf. It's too large and too dark to be a coyote."

"I doubt it," Father said. "And even if it is a wolf, it's more interested in the colts than us."

Verna and I began to whimper about the danger to the colts. "Don't worry," Mother said. "God protected us from those big horses, and he'll watch over the colts."

I sensed the strength of my parents' faith and felt comforted. We settled back down beneath the Irish blanket as the sun hovered over the horizon. Jackrabbits bounded in and out of view. A shadow swept over the team and buggy, cast by a massive hawk. He chased a rabbit toward us, and I feared in its terror it would dash under the wheels. At the last second, it changed direction and fled. The hawk swooped low and struck out with its talons, but the rabbit darted off at an angle. The hawk attacked again, and then again. Each time, the rabbit escaped. At last, the bird gave up the hunt and flew off in a long slant toward the setting sun.

The team brought us back to the hogbacks, and Father pulled the horses to a walk for the rocky, difficult traverse. Cravens Flat spread out before us, a checkerboard of bright green fields of winter wheat, brown plowed squares ready for planting, and green pastures. Dusty ribbons of road edged the section lines and dipped out of sight at Skene Hill. The fenced fields of Craven Flat were evidence of man's conquest of a good earth ripe with promise and beauty.

"What a contrast to the wild land we have just come over," said Mother. "How peaceful and welcoming it looks."

"In this light it looks as rich and green as Ireland," said Father. "But, no, the fence lines are too square and the fields are much larger. Some day the prairies will all be like this. Little by little man will accomplish it."

Mother linked her arm with Father's. "I'm glad we're a part of it."

"I hope it isn't much farther. I've got pins and needles in my feet." I stretched out a leg and tried to wiggle a numb foot.

"Me too," said Verna, and began kicking her dangling heels against the base of the buggy seat.

"Just be patient a little longer," said Mother. "Rub your foot to wake it up, Lenna."

The next moment, the buggy topped the hill. Below lay Edgemont, blanketed in the grey shadow of dusk. The red switch lights along the railroad tracks winked as we descended into town.

Chapter 5

The Wild West

Father blew in the back door, past Mother, Verna, and me sitting at the kitchen table shelling the few burned up pea pods we'd managed to harvest. Without saying a word, he stormed out the front, slamming the screen door behind him. "I declare," Mother said. "I believe the heat's finally got to him."

The heat and drought that first summer was hard for all of us to bear. The blazing sun scorched and eventually killed the small garden Father had made in the backyard. The cucumber vine by the front porch hung lifeless on the climbing strings Father had put up. The tireless wind rattled the cottonwood trees and sent hot blasts through the screen doors and around the drawn blinds of the houses. Whirlwinds dancing down the dusty streets tossed dirty papers along the wooden sidewalks.

I raced after Father, determined to find out what had gotten him so riled up. I caught up with him at the mayor's garden gate. Mr. Dale's house was neat and freshly painted and a woven wire fence surrounded his carefully tended yard and garden.

"Mayor Dale," Father said.

Mr. Dale, a short, round man with a white mustache, was bent over, hoeing his beds. He craned his head without interrupting his cultivating. "Good morning, Reverend O'Neill. Going to be another scorcher. Hard on the plants. Thought I'd try to help them through the day." The Dale place was an oasis among the wind-dried, bare yards of the neighborhood. To water a lawn enough so it would survive a hot, dry summer required more time, effort, and water than most people could spare. But Mr. Dale worked in his yard every morning and evening, and his cinnamon pinks were the most fragrant flowers I'd ever smelled. I had learned to stand outside the fence, watching and talking politely until he'd give me a single spicy flower.

"Good morning, sir," Father said. "Beautiful flowers, yes, but have you heard about the shooting?" Mr. Dale solemnly plucked a pink flower and handed it to me, and then, leaning on his hoe, looked intently at Father.

"Is something wrong, Reverend?"

Father's voice rose. "Mr. Frost was shot not two hours ago. I wonder that you haven't heard."

"I heard something about it." Mr. Dale poked at a recalcitrant weed with his hoe. "Just what did happen?"

"I was told he was involved in a card game over in Luck a few days ago and won a huge sum from Pfeister. Supposedly, there was a woman involved too. Anyway, early this morning Pfeister rode into town roaring drunk and sent word to Frost he was coming to kill him. Frost came down the stairs with his guns on, but Pfeister didn't give him a chance. Shot him as he opened the door!"

"I suppose the sheriff was called," Mr. Dale said. He leaned against the hoe and swayed.

"No. Pfeister got back on his horse and rode out of town. I suppose if he reaches the state line, nothing will be done about it." I'd heard all about outlaw country just ten miles away across the line in Wyoming where the hills and ravines hid gunmen and rustlers from the law.

"But what about Frost?"

"I suppose being shot through the wrist is better than losing your life, but what if he can't continue his dentistry?" Father slapped his thigh. "It's 1913! Why isn't something being done about this lawlessness?"

Mr. Dale leaned his hoe against the fence. "Mr. O'Neill, we're really doing well here. Only a few years back, shootings and killings were common. I carried my guns all the time. Now, I can go unarmed. There's seldom any gunplay. We're improving. Give us time."

Father's fists rested on his hips, and his voice was as loud as Mayor Dale's was calm and quiet. "I don't call it much improvement when the town is filled with saloons and gambling houses. I hear one of our saloons is known throughout the Black Hills as a fence for stolen goods. Has anything ever been done about that, sir?"

I had never heard father raise his voice to anyone, and I hadn't seen him this angry since the funeral of an Edgemont man killed in an argument over range rights. It had been out-and-out murder, yet no murder charge was made. There was a brief obituary in the weekly newspaper, but that was all. Though Father had been outraged, he'd kept his feelings inside the family.

Mayor Dale's pleasant smile disappeared. "Getting law enforcement in this town is a slow process, but we'll get it. He grabbed his hoe. "I'm due at a meeting. Thanks for your interest, Reverend. Good day."

A few weeks later, when the water mains were put in, workers dug up a skeleton right in front of the parsonage. To Father's horror, the bones were thrown into a box and taken to the town dump.

"No telling who it was," he said when he complained to the sheriff.

"Might have been an Indian. No use worrying about it," the sheriff said. "Sorry, Reverend. I can't waste my time worrying over someone who's been dead no telling how long."

Even if they were buried in the cemetery, some people never got a proper funeral. Sometimes the body was taken to the cemetery and buried with no ceremony whatsoever. "It's not Christian!" Father protested, but nothing ever came of his complaints.

Mr. Bartlett, who owned the general store, tried to settle Father down with a story that only made him feel worse about living among such irreverent people.

"On a bitter, cold winter day," Mr. Bartlett said, "a home-steader drove to town in his lumber wagon. He tied the team in front of one of the saloons and went in to warm himself. Many drinks later, he said to his companions at the bar, 'Must go get a box for the old lady.'

"He staggered over to my store and said he needed the cheapest burial box in stock. 'Got the old lady out in the wagon. She died last week, but I couldn't get to town until now because of the snow. She kept good because it's been so cold.'" Sure enough, I found the dead woman, frozen solid, wrapped in a blanket in the back of the wagon. Beside her lay two hairless, butchered hogs, also frozen. He'd brought them along to sell.

"The old coot went back to the saloon and, after a few more drinks, recruited three of his drinking buddies to help him. They headed out to the cemetery in their own lumber wagon, and tried to pass the homesteader with his dead wife and the hogs. The homesteader stubbornly refused to let them by. The two teams raced along the road, over the frozen ruts, the hogs and the pine box bouncing around in the wagon. After the burial, the men went back to the saloon and entertained everyone with their story. Never did hear what happened to the hogs."

"What a terrible story," Father said with a strained smile.

One blistering early summer day a neighbor stopped by the parsonage. "Better keep your doors locked. Just heard there's a mad man loose. James Sykes from out Provo way has been missing since about midnight. Threatened to kill his family and then left. They think he's headed for town."

"We know him," Mother said. "His family attends our Provo church services. How awful!"

All that day we kept our screen doors locked, and no one answered the door but Father. Then Mrs. Sykes's sister came to our house. The poor woman was shaken. Her red face gleamed with sweat. "They found him wandering on the prairie barefoot in his nightshirt. He had wandered several miles from home and was down toward the Stanford hogbacks. His poor feet are full of cactus thorns, and he's terribly sunburned. They had to handcuff him to bring him in. You know what a strong, big man he is. He's sick. Out of his head." Tears puddled on her fat cheeks. "They've got him in jail," she wailed.

Father went to the jail with her to see what he could do to help. But it was much later, after Mr. Sykes had become unconscious and raved no longer, that the doctor determined that he had typhoid fever, not insanity.

Father fumed. "Are the sheriff's men stupid, ignorant, or both? Imagine, treating a sick man that way."

His gentleness and sensitivity made him vulnerable and impractical sometimes, but we knew how stubborn and determined he could be and how much the troubles of the town upset him. Rudeness and profanity could be forgiven, but the fistfights, drunkenness, gun battles—the disregard for humanity and justice—shattered him. We knew he did more than prepare for his Sunday sermons in his study. He spent hours on his knees praying for help to meet the challenges of this community. Despite Father's efforts to civilize the town, life in Edgemont went on just as it always had.

Eventually Father's mood lightened. By the end of the summer, he began to sleep more regularly and that made him feel better. Church filled up on Sundays despite the rampant lawlessness. The more permanent people—the depot agent, the dispatcher, the roundhouse men, and their families—came to church. The cattle ranchers and sheep men may have heard about the new preacher in town, but we didn't see them at the services. The homesteaders, clinging to the land with hope for a more so-called cultured tomorrow, most sincerely welcomed us. People came from surrounding areas to hear the Irish preacher tell of the Bible and God's love. In his sermons, he reminded them God helped those who helped themselves and suggested they help themselves with better law enforcement.

Chapter 6

The Circus and Buffalo Bill

Buffalo Bill

B y late July, the summer began to burn itself out. Bright-colored posters on walls and light posts announced the arrival of the world-famous Sells-Floto Circus. We all talked about it. Everyone planned to attend.

"Well, girlies, your father met a famous man this morning," Father announced at supper. "Guess who?"

"Tell us, Papa. Who?" Verna and I cried in unison.

"You'll never guess, Dearie," he said to mother. "As I was passing the Goddard house on my way home just now, Mr. Goddard called, 'Come on up here, Reverend O'Neill. I want you to meet a friend of mine.'"

"When I got up on the porch and out of the bright sunlight, I saw a handsome man with flowing white hair. I should have recognized him from the posters but couldn't think for a minute where I'd seen him before. It was Mr. William Cody or Buffalo Bill as he's called. He and Mr. Goddard are old friends. He came ahead of the circus for a short visit with them. They were railroad scouts together when they were young men. Imagine that!"

"So that's why the circus is stopping here?" Mother asked.

"Mr. Goddard had fun telling him about my being a green Irishman trying to make cowboys into angels. Mr. Cody laughed and said he wished me luck but didn't think I'd have much."

"Is that long white hair and that fancy beard real?" Mother questioned.

"Yes. I think so. He's a handsome man, loud and rough, though. He's much older than the posters show. And, girls, look at these free tickets for the circus. Buffalo Bill gave them to me himself. Isn't that wonderful?"

The next morning, the circus trains were on the siding down by the roundhouse. Nearly everyone in town went down to watch the unloading. There were three trains, each with many coaches. It took one train just to haul the circus performers and the workmen. More than a city block at the north edge of town had been cleared for the big tent and other tents and wagons.

"I do believe that train has nothing but horses," Mother said as we watched the matched teams come down the wooden ramps from the railroad cards. "Look at those beautiful, big dapple grays—eight of them—exactly alike."

"This circus is especially famous for its horses," Father said. "What beauties! Look at those chestnuts and the sorrels. And those dainty black ponies—there must be twenty of them!"

We pointed and commented and gasped with pleasure as the horses kept on coming. There were Indian pintos, Arabians, matched white carriage ponies, huge draft horses with ribbons braided into their manes and the long hair above their hoofs washed snowy white. There were tall, graceful cream-colored horses, spotted ponies, and roans. Many were working, hitched to the cages, carriages, circus wagons, and the calliope. We watched all morning, and when we went home at noon, we could see the big brown circus tent billowing in the wind out at the edge of town.

At one o'clock, we watched the circus parade from the top step of White's store on Main Street. Buffalo Bill rode at the head of the parade in a carriage pulled by white horses with gold-colored plumes in their bridles and gold tassels on their harnesses. Mr. Goddard sat beside Buffalo Bill, and when they came opposite us, Mr. Goddard waved at our family, and

Buffalo Bill, wearing the fringed leather suit and the white Stetson shown in all the circus posters, lifted a gauntlet-gloved hand to my father.

Buffalo Bill's famous white horse followed behind the carriage. Gold-colored medallions shone like yellow sunflowers on the straps across the chest and forehead of the tall horse and silver studs and ornaments on the saddle glittered in the sunlight. I wished the famous man was on his horse instead of in the carriage. In the posters, the two of them looked so proud and grand.

I was so excited and interested I almost missed seeing the blue and silver calliope pass by, little plums of steam dancing from pipe to pipe with the melody.

There were ladies in white tights and fluffy skirts doing dance steps on the broad backs of the dapple gray horses. The tiny black ponies pulled a gilded cage with a lion in it. Elephants walked ponderously by carrying brightly costumed men on gleaming thrones. The tiny, dark men crossed their arms and stared straight ahead, oblivious to the crowd. Cage after cage of jungle animals rumbled down the street followed by a red and gold wagon with the circus band atop playing a jubilant march.

Indians, looking much cleaner and more brightly dressed than those who came to town from the Pine Ridge, whooped as they galloped by on their pintos. They hooked a knee over the horse's back and slid sideways to use the horse's body as a shield from an imaginary foe. Then they righted themselves and shot an imaginary arrow into the crowd before whirling back into the parade again.

We all followed the parade to the big tent and joined the crowds watching the caged animals and the roustabouts watering and cleaning the horses and elephants. Our family walked right by the man waving his cane and beseeching the people to "Buy your tickets right here for the greatest show of all, The Sells-Floto, world acclaimed, just back from a tour of the romantic continent!" We gave our complimentary tickets to an usher who pointed to seats near the center ring. The wooden planks weren't very comfortable, and the tent didn't look as glamorous as I had imagined, but it didn't matter once the band began to play. The show was on!

Buffalo Bill and his white horse came slowly around the ring, cantering in time to the music. He held his gloved hand high in a salute and smiled out over the crowd. The people responded by rising, clapping, and cheering as he went by. Verna and I clapped as hard as we could. I stood up on the plank seat, hoping to get another glimpse of the famous man, but he didn't come around the ring again. Instead, he stopped his horse at the entrance. The horse knelt gracefully, and Buffalo Bill took off his Stetson and bowed low to us all.

Buffalo Bill left the ring, and suddenly, there were so many things going on, it was hard to know what to watch. The best part was when horses and men, all painted white, made tableaus or living statues, the horses trained to stand so still they seemed not to breathe.

There were cowboy-and-Indian scenes with a mock raid on a covered wagon. There was a stagecoach holdup and trick riding and lassoing. A cowboy riding behind an Indian who threw glass balls in the air shot every ball to smithereens before the pieces fell to the sawdust floor. A lady in a fringed costume shot a cigarette out of a man's mouth and then outlined his body with bullet holes as he stood bravely before a wooden door.

Lions and tigers in wire cages performed tricks when a man holding a chair cracked his whip. The band played loudly, except when the trapeze artists performed in the top of the tent, or the lady walked the tightrope. There were clowns, balloons, popcorn, and always the wonderful horses.

The performances flew by in a great blur. Before I knew it, the band played a grand finale and the circus was over.

"Did you see that clown that had feet like a duck?" Verna asked as we struggled through the crowd toward the door.

"Yes," I said. "But did you see that lady slip off the horse she was standing on as it galloped around the ring? She jumped right back up again and was still standing up as she rode on. I wonder how she learned to do that. And those little black horses! I wish I could have a black horse someday."

We talked about the circus for days afterward. It was my first circus, and none after ever compared.

Chapter 7

Outlaw Country

"Lenna, would you like to go to Clifton with me next Sunday?" Mother said. "Last time Verna got so terrified at the mice and pack rats in that sod house. I think she'd rather stay home. Right, Verna?"

Verna nodded doubtfully, and I shouted with glee. I hadn't been on a train since the night we came to Edgemont.

"Let's hope a different family offers us a place to stay this time," Mother said.

As one of the few women ordained in the ministry, Mother was able to help Father when he had too many places to be at once. By the spring of 1914, they were preaching in four small outlying communities. There were no regular salaries at these places, just small offerings. After paying train fares or the cost of a hired livery team, there was little money left. But profit was not important to my parents. They felt they must go wherever people needed them.

They held regular twice-a-month Sunday afternoon services in Provo and also preached in Driftwood, Clifton, Dewey, and Moss Agate at irregular intervals. Edgemont, of course, had a morning and evening service every Sunday.

The next Saturday, Mother and I rode the train to the outlaw country over the Wyoming state line. My eyes grew heavy watching the barren, gray land whiz by. The sun was setting as we pulled into Clifton, which was not much more than a flag stop along the Burlington line. There were no houses in town. A few dotted the foothills, far apart from each other. I thought about the rats in the sod house and shuddered.

A young man, probably in his early twenties, met us at the station and drove us in his spring wagon to a rude claim house a couple of miles up the road.

An older woman, surely in her forties, stood in the doorway. "Meet the wife," he said. "We ain't got much, but what's ours, you're welcome to."

The young man said little all evening. He hunched over, elbows on the table and kept his face turned away from us. The woman, on the other hand, talked and talked.

"Did you hear? They found the bones of that Jones boy and his horse that went down in the quicksand last summer."

Mother gave me a quick glance and said she hadn't heard.

"He saddled a pony and set out for town, but he never made it. They figured the quicksand got him when he tried to ford the river. Sure enough, after that last cloudburst, the flood uncovered the bones."

Mother made a polite comment. I could tell she didn't want to encourage any more storytelling.

"The wolves are what scare me," the woman went on. "Last winter a pack of them chased four deer right up to the house and killed a doe right before our eyes. That's why we got that gun hanging so handy."

The husband finally spoke up. "Tell her about the Spencer's runaway last winter."

"Oh, yes! The Spencers—they're pretty old—they'd gone to Dewey for groceries. In winter, the folks hereabout often use the river ice for road. The Spencers were leaving the ice when a wolf scared the team. The team ran, strewed the groceries every which way, then broke loose and went on home."

The young man perked up at this point and watched his wife intently, his eyes gleaming and a thin smile crossing his lips.

"Ma Spencer ended up with a broken leg," she went on. "The wolves knew it, I guess. They hung around in the timber just waiting."

The young man broke in, animated no doubt by the terrifying tale. "Pa Spencer struggled with the wagon box and finally got it turned upside down. He set Ma Spencer under it, and there she stayed, while he went for help. He figured it would be some time before them critters dug through the ice and snow to get at her."

Mother glanced over at me. My eyes were like marbles in my head. I barely breathed as I focused on every word.

"Pa Spencer was right," the woman said. "He was hurt some and it took awhile for him to get up to Matteson's, but practically all them ten kids and Mr. Matteson came back with him, and they got the wagon turned back up and the team hitched again. They had the old lady up to their house in no time. Could have been a different story, if it hadn't been daylight, or if the wolves had got under the wagon. I shudder to think."

"It's nice visiting this way, but my little girl is awfully tired," Mother said. "Would you mind if we went to our room?"

The woman led us to a small bedroom. Red roses climbed up the papered walls and a red and blue braided rug covered the floor beside the iron bed. No sign of sod dust or rat turds, to my relief. The woman set a kerosene lamp on the washstand by the bed. "We have a terrible time with bedbugs." She pointed at tin cans cupping each leg of the bed. "There's kerosene in them. Keeps the bedbugs from crawling up into the bed. Hope you sleep good."

I was a girl who practically lived outdoors. I didn't mind bugs a bit, and I'd never heard of bedbugs. The long train ride and the soft featherbed sent me to sleep as soon as Mother blew out the lamp.

"Lenna, get out of bed." Mother woke me and pulled me up.

I scrambled out of bed. Mother lit the lamp and threw back the covers. Several small reddish-brown bugs scurried away from the light into the folds of the bedding. Mother placed the lamp on the washstand, snatched off the bottom sheet and shook it hard. Then she held up the light again and peered all along the edges of the featherbed. She found more bugs and dropped them into the lamp chimney. They sizzled and smoked and sent up a horrible odor like the stink of rotten eggs on fire. I held my nose while she checked each sheet and quilt and made up the bed again. She inspected the pillows and pillowcases the same way. This time, when we climbed back into bed, she left the lamp burning.

Before my eyes even closed, Mother whispered, "Look at the ceiling, Lenna."

A tiny speck dropped from the ceiling to the bed, and then another. Mother jumped up, caught the two bedbugs and dropped them in the lamp chimney. She held the lamp high, under lots more bugs crawling on the ceiling. They lost their grip and met their fiery death in the hot chimney, one by one. Mother walked back and forth, the length of the room, with the burning trap until she had covered the entire ceiling. Then she sat down on the bed to rest.

"Those nasty, clever bugs learned how to evade the kerosene," she said, looking up in awe. "Maybe we'll get so sleepy we won't notice their pinches."

We must have been pretty tired. The woman had to pound on the door to wake us the next morning. Mother warned me not to mention the bugs. She said the poor woman was surely doing her best to keep a clean house in this rough place.

I noticed the man and woman hardly spoke to each other at breakfast. He left the house early to do chores and stayed gone all morning.

When he came back, his wife scolded him. "Why can't you be on time for once? You know we have to have an early dinner to be at the church service by one-thirty. Where you been anyway?"

"None of your business," he growled.

"Sneakin' around with that girl again. In the morning yet." Her voice rose. "What a fool you are."

"Woman, ain't you got no sense at all?"

"Now, now—" Mother broke in. The woman whirled around and hissed at Mother. "He ain't no good. I married me a no-count boy that thinks of nothin' but that Maynard girl."

Mother and I backed away. I sucked in my breath and felt mother grasp my hand.

The woman's eyes blazed, and her face burned bright red. "I have half a notion to blow his brains out and be done with him!"

She took a shotgun down from the wall and began rummaging around in a drawer. "Damn! Where are those shells?"

"Hattie, calm down. Ain't no shells for the gun and you're the fool. Get dinner on the table and shut your mouth."

Hattie looked defeated, like a flag on a pole when the wind's died down. She shuffled back and forth from the stove to the table. When we were all seated, Mother said grace in a tight voice, and we began to eat the boiled potatoes and limp greens Hattie had fixed for us. My stomach churned, and

I choked down the food. The room descended into a cold silence.

At the church service, I sat in front with the other children, far from Hattie and her young husband. Mother stumbled through the sermon. Her hands trembled when she held her Bible to read the scripture.

On the train, Mother asked me if the yelling and fighting had frightened me. I said no, but really, it had. It scared me too to see Mother's hand shaking like that and realize that my invincible mother could be afraid. I felt like we'd come through something together, and I'd grown up a little in that short trip.

Mother never went back and neither did I. From then on, Father had to go to Clifton on his own.

Chapter 8

Mother's Kindergarten

(left to right) Verna and Lenna O'Neill

By late summer, the other children my age were getting ready to start kindergarten, but Mother wanted to keep me home. She didn't think the streets of Edgemont were safe for me. Many days cattle took them over as cowboys drove them to the stockyards, where they penned them before loading them onto the trains. Afterward the cowboys went to the darkened saloons. At all hours, rough, drunk men spilled out of the swinging doors into the light.

Mother visited with the school superintendent and argued that we lived farther from the big sandstone school building than most children, and I wouldn't be of school age until January, and there were no older children in our neighborhood to help me safely to and from school.

She showed him her second-grade teaching certificate that she'd earned before going to Chicago to become a minister. Apparently that clinched the deal, and she was given permission to teach me at home. Before long, neighbors were asking Mother to teach their preschool children. By the end of September, ten children, including Verna and me, were attending kindergarten at our house.

Though the parsonage was small, it had a third bedroom Father used for his study and a parlor that we didn't need during the day. Mother convinced Father he wouldn't be too badly disturbed, and he helped her turn the parlor into a classroom. He got out his carpenter tools and made low benches and tables, which he painted bright red to Verna's and my delight.

For five days a week, from nine to eleven each morning, Mother had her little school. Fifty cents from each child earned her four dollars a week. Considering the low salary Father was paid, Mother's earnings helped a great deal.

Mother believed in drills to teach us words and numbers. Many an evening Verna and I helped make flash cards with any usable cardboard we could find. We traced pictures and colored them in with crayons. One of our chief delights was folding colored construction paper into chickens, boxes, stars, and other shapes. Mother made learning fun, but she was a strict disciplinarian. Nevertheless, we knew she loved us all.

One morning in October, Verna and I went to play at the nearby home of a schoolmate named Ruthie Lee. When we went out to play in the yard, she said, "We mustn't be too noisy. Mrs. Elder is sick. The doctor brought her a new baby last night." Verna and I looked over at the house next door and at each other. I raised an eyebrow, but I let Ruthie go on. I knew, and I knew Verna knew that there was something wrong with that story. "I saw him bring it in a satchel," she said, wide-eyed and busting with pride.

"A satchel?" Verna said, voicing her disbelief.

"Doctors don't bring babies to mothers," I said in a scornful tone. "They grow inside the mother and come out a hole in her body."

"They do not. I saw the doctor bring the baby in the satchel," Ruthie said. "Anyway, how could they get inside the mother to come out?"

"I don't know all the particulars, but my mother told me babies come just like puppies do—out of a hole in the mother." I assumed I could end the argument with this statement of fact.

"It isn't so," Ruthie cried. "We'll go ask my mother."

The three of us stomped into the house.

"Didn't the doctor come with his satchel and bring Mrs. Elder's baby?" Ruthie said, sounding very sure of herself.

"Yes, dear. Isn't that wonderful?" Mrs. Lee said.

"But my mother says babies come out of a hole in the mother," I said, standing my ground.

Mrs. Lee gasped. She dropped the roll she was shaping and eyed us like we needed a good whipping. "I think you O'Neill girls should go home at once."

Verna and I looked at each other in dismay. Neither of us had expected this turn of events, but we obeyed. We kicked at the dusty street before breaking into a slow run. At our garden gate, Verna said, "Wonder why Mrs. Lee didn't know about babies better than that."

We went out back to the chicken coop, which we'd made into a playhouse, though we shared it with the hens. Some time later, Mother called me in.

At the back door, I heard Mrs. Lee's voice and paused on the stoop, out of sight. "You understand, Mrs. O'Neill, we just can't have our children learning those things this way. Under the circumstances we feel that we must withdraw from your school. We thought it only fair to come and tell you why."

"There must be some mistake," Mother said. "I can't believe my girls would talk in a smutty way." The boards creaked under my feet. Thinking I'd be discovered eavesdropping, I went on in.

"There you are, Lenna." She introduced me to two women I didn't know, mothers of two of my schoolmates. "Of course, you know Mrs. Lee." I curtsied, just as she'd taught me, and stood at attention next to Mother.

"Please tell me what you girls were talking about when you were playing with Ruthie this morning," Mother said.

Mother's eyebrows crossed the way they did when she was angry about something. I gazed at the ladies in their hats and best dresses. One of the ladies kept wiping her face with her handkerchief and looking down at the floor. The other one smiled, but her eyes were cold and sharp. Mrs. Lee pressed her lips into a thin line and stared at me like a bird of prey.

If Mother hadn't reached out and put an arm around me, I surely would have run. My heart pounded in my ears.

Verna banged the back door behind her and came to a short stop at the sight of the gathering. Her dress and hands were caked with mud, and her jaw dropped at the sight of all the grim faces. She sidled next to me.

"Verna, these ladies have come to see us about something you girls said at Ruthie's this morning. Lenna is about to tell us," Mother said.

My mind went blank. I couldn't imagine what they wanted to know. That may be why I couldn't find any words when I opened my mouth to speak.

"Just tell us what you were talking about," Mother said.

"Yes, and tell the truth," Mrs. Lee said.

"She will," Mother promised. "Go ahead, Lenna."

I thought back to the baby in the satchel and pictured Mrs. Lee's angry face when she sent us home.

"Well, Ruthie was telling us about Mrs. Elder's new baby coming in a satchel."

I couldn't get a breath and my mouth dried up, but somehow, I spit it out. "I told her babies didn't come from doctors, and she got mad."

The ladies' cheeks got very red, and I heard a gasp escape from one of them. I felt like I'd better defend myself, so I hurried on. "I tried to explain that babies come out of the mother, like you said, but she wouldn't listen. When we went into the house, Mrs. Lee told us to go home." My knees got so quivery, they shook my whole body.

"Is that all you said?" Mother asked.

"I think so."

"We told her babies came just like Queen's puppies, only not five," Verna said with an emphatic nod.

"Thank you, girls," Mother said. "Go on back outside."

Later, I found Mother in the kitchen peeling potatoes for supper. "Are Tommy and Mary and Ruth coming back to school?"

"Oh, I think they'll come to school tomorrow all right. Mrs. Lee didn't understand what you said to Ruthie. She thought you said something bad." She pumped some water at the sink and rinsed the potatoes in the colander. "However, I think it would be best not to talk to other children about babies being born. We'll just let their mothers tell them. If we know the truth about it, that's enough. All right?" I didn't really feel relieved until she dried her hands on her apron and gathered me in a hug.

At supper, Father said, "Girls, always remember who you are. Be careful not to shame yourself or our family. Being the preacher's daughters will never be easy. You'll be expected to behave better than everybody else, and if you do or don't, everybody will be watching and waiting to criticize."

That sounded like one of his sermons to me. I didn't understand until years later, after I'd done quite a few things right and wrong. But one thing I knew for sure, then and always: Mother and Father loved us and would stand by us no matter what.

Chapter 9

The Homestead

Heat and drought, howling winds and driving blizzards, lawlessness and uppity ladies didn't send Mother and Father packing, but in the fall of 1914, a scourge descended upon Edgemont, and by the spring of 1915, my parents made plans to move on.

Verna came down with the whooping cough first. Mother tried to prevent the terrible choking spells at night by waking her every hour or two. I caught it next and coughed so much I couldn't hold down any food. I grew weaker by the day and wanted to sleep the winter through, but Verna wouldn't let me be. The epidemic closed down our school. Most of the children in the community were stricken. One child died. As I grew stronger, Father succumbed. Mother nursed him and helped with the church work through the winter. But Father's poor health and services in four different communities were wearing both of them out.

Dr. Thompson warned Father he'd have a breakdown if he didn't withdraw from all his commitments and get some rest. The doctor's nurse knew how ill Father was, and she had a prescription. "Why don't you folks take a homestead and earn a home while Reverend O'Neill is regaining his health?"

she said. She told them about the Sykes, her relatives in Provo who were about to lose their homestead. The parcel lay in the midst of the open range where Walter Cavinder grazed his sheep. "Reverend, buy that land before Cavinder knows it's relinquished."

Everyone knew and feared the land-hungry Cavinder. He had used the open range around Provo to graze his sheep for years, but homesteaders were fencing the open land, and he bitterly resented them, doing all manner of mischief to drive them away. He would snatch the land if someone didn't file for it first.

Mother shook her head. "I'm afraid he's not strong enough to do farm work."

"If your husband continues his public work here, he'll never get well," Dr. Thompson said.

There was little time to ponder. Before the week was out, James Sykes signed the papers relinquishing the 160 acres, making it government land once more. At the same time, Father paid him $160 and filed claim to the land.

The property had no buildings on it. For fifty dollars, my parents bought a twelve-by-fourteen-foot house covered in tar paper and a barn, which church members helped move onto our homestead.

Now Mother and Father had a predicament. We were required to live at least six months of each year on the land and make improvements in order to hold on to the claim. But all their money had gone for the purchase of the relinquishment and the buildings. The Edgemont church was their only source of income. For awhile at least, they would have to continue preaching there.

Once the buildings were moved, life returned to normal. We were gathered around the table for supper one night, and Mother and Father were talking about the big move to Provo. "If only we had an automobile," Mother said.

"Well, that's impossible," Father said. "We can't afford it."

Not for the first or the last time, Mother's wishes prevailed. On the first of April, we packed all our belongings into our new Model T Ford and headed out to our new home in Provo. My father thought the automobile was the work of the Lord, but I thought Mother had a lot to do with it.

She had returned from the post office one afternoon near the end of March and practically danced into Father's study. "Oh, Joe. Look at this." We followed close behind, curious to know what she was waving around that made her so excited.

"Mrs. Magna has sent us money!" That got Father's full attention.

"Listen," Mother said, and she read the letter aloud. "'I shared your letter about the homestead with our church guild. As you know, we have all taken great interest in you and your family, and we earnestly wish to help you in this new undertaking. Since transportation to and from the homestead will determine whether or not Reverend O'Neill can continue serving in the Edgemont church, the Holyoke guild is sending you the enclosed check, which will help defray the cost of an automobile.'"

Father stared at the check in disbelief. "The Lord is with us!"

Our new Model T carried us and our belongings through blossoming prairies up Skene Hill, across the hogbacks, and onto the flatland of Provo. A lane was yet to be carved into the grassland, so we bounced and jounced to our one-room house and barn at the north edge of the claim.

Though our house was rough and tiny, it was well built, including a good roof and two windows. The walls had big holes where plaster had fallen off in the moving, and there were signs of bedbugs. Mother tackled these problems with zest. She purchased creosote oil, mixed it with flour and water, and fastened layer after layer of newspaper over the holes in the lath walls. Over this she pasted squares of old torn sheets and cotton blankets. When this was dry and smooth, she covered the wall and ceiling with cheap but cheerful wallpaper. She filled every crevice and crack around windows and woodwork with the paste containing the creosote bedbug poison.

"It's no disgrace to have bedbugs in this country," said Mrs. Cass as she watched Mother put poison along the floor edge one day, "it's just a disgrace to have too many. It's a hopeless fight. Everybody's got them."

"Well, we're not going to have them if I can help it," Mother declared.

Our furniture was brought from Edgemont in a lumber wagon. We didn't need or have room for much. Mother bought a small iron cookstove for five dollars. She curtained off one corner for a closet, and Father built some shelves for dishes. We girls slept on a metal cot with sides that folded down during the day, and Father and Mother slept on a folding bed, the most imposing item in the room. By day, it looked like a bureau with drawer pulls, and at night, its straw mattress unfolded like a jackknife. A drop-leaf table and four chairs sat under one of the windows. Mother's sewing machine, a rocking chair, and a brass-bound trunk filled with books and magazines like *McCall's* and *Youth's Companion* completed our furnishings.

During those first weeks, Father was busy with hammer and saw. He built a doorstep and a lean-to kitchen. At one end of the lean-to, he built a bin to store coal and kindling. He made a wide door in one side of the barn so the car could be sheltered inside.

Verna and I explored our new yard—the wide prairie all around us. We discovered tadpoles and clinging snails in the rain-filled water holes of the grassy wash and found glistening crystals in the rocks along the gully ledges. We played house in the tall weeds and buffalo grass. When we found unusual plants and blossoming cactuses, we dug them up and replanted them in tin cans. Queen had two puppies, and the three collies accompanied Verna and me wherever we went.

Mother loved to read, and on the days when Father was in Edgemont all day studying or taking care of church business, she read to us from the store of magazines in the trunk. School started again once we were settled, and she spent hours teaching us to read and do simple arithmetic.

It was a happy time for us all. Though the house was tiny, we had much more freedom. At last we girls didn't have to tiptoe around during the day. Father was sleeping better than he had for years and the cough was almost gone. I was confident this happiness would go on forever, but Mr. Cavinder had other ideas.

Chapter 10

The Sheep

The Model T had just disappeared across the prairie with Father at the wheel heading for Edgemont when we heard the beat of horse's hoofs. We watched the rider trot along the fence north of the house. He dismounted, opened the wire gate, got back on his horse, and rode right up to our door. He pulled up the reins of his chestnut gelding at our stoop.

He kept his Stetson on and stared at Mother with hard blue eyes, as the sun at his back cast a shadow over us. The straight line of his thick lips, half hidden beneath a bristly brown mustache, didn't curve into a smile.

"I'm Cavinder," he said. "I want to talk to the preacher."

The horse chewed on its curb bit and backed away. Cavinder spurred him forward again. I feared he would ride right through our doorway.

Mother didn't move.

"I'm sorry. He's not here," she said in a pleasant tone that defied his malevolent stance.

"You tell him he's to get off this land. He's not an American citizen, and he's got no right to this land." He spit on the ground at our feet. "You folks better get back to town before you have some real trouble. Tell him that."

He turned his horse, gave him a quick kick of the spurs and galloped in the direction from which he'd come. His brown shirt billowed, making him look even bigger than he was.

Mother stared after him for a minute. Then she strode out and closed the gate, giving it an angry shove. We knew Cavinder had terrorized many of our neighbors. He was determined to get rid of us any way he could.

We watched a large herd of sheep follow a covered wagon along the top of the rise. The sheepherder's wagon stayed on the government land, but eventually, the sheep wandered down to our homestead. Our barbed wire fence didn't stop them. Thick, white wool covered the lower wires as they traveled back and forth beneath the barbs. The sound of their bleating and the occasional barking of the herder's dogs kept Queen pacing and panting. Mother remained outwardly calm, but Verna and I both saw the worry in her face.

We watched the sheep and the wagon all day long. We ignored our studies, staying on the stoop or inside. A while before sunset, Queen bristled. She stood stiff-legged and growling in the doorway. Mother stayed behind the screen door, and we stayed behind her. I watched the sheepherder approach with my heart in my throat. He was unshaven and poorly dressed, but unlike Cavinder, he took off his hat and nodded in greeting.

"Lady, could I have a drink?"

"Yes," Mother said. "Help yourself from the rain barrel."

The man kept his gaze on Mother for a moment before lowering his eyes. He turned to the rain barrel just outside the door, lifted the dipper from its hook, and took a sip of water. "Thanks," he said, looking back up at Mother in a slow, vaguely threatening way. He whistled for his dogs and sent them to round up the sheep, following them back out the gate. Mother unhooked the dipper and took it inside to clean. Within half an hour, the sheep and wagon disappeared over the rise.

That night, my parents talked long after dark about citizenship for Father. He had come to America in 1905, but he did not apply for citizenship until 1910, after taking Mother and me to Ireland for a visit. By law, Mother and I were considered aliens like Father, and when we returned from Ireland, we had to go through Ellis Island, just as all foreigners did. After that, Mother couldn't stand the thought that she was no longer an American. She urged Father to apply for citizenship. He'd applied for and received his first papers, but when the time came for him to take out the second and final papers, he'd procrastinated.

Father understood he must become a citizen within three years of filing his claim on the homestead. There had been no question about the first papers being in order when he had filed his claim. Did Cavinder know something that we did not? If he was planning to use Father's lack of citizenship as a means of getting us off the land, Mother and Father were determined to disappoint him.

Mother wrote to Hot Springs asking for a date when Father could appear before the judge. When the answer came, Father learned that unless he applied for the final papers before the end of the month, his application for citizenship would be void, and he would have to apply all over again.

"Now we know why Cavinder was so insolent," Father said. "He thought I would file too late and not have citizenship when it came time to prove up on the land. Well, I'm going to outsmart him!"

The next day, Dad Jahns stopped by on his way back from Provo. Twice a week his bent but spry figure crossed the pasture below our house as he walked to town to get the mail and groceries. Over his shoulder he always carried his "snakewhip," a piece of broomstick with a wire attached. At the end of the wire was a large machinery nut. A collection of rattlesnake rattles attested to his skill with this weapon, and he loved to pull a handful of rattles from his pocket, describe the snake in detail, and tell the exact date on which the battle had occurred.

Jahns was our nearest neighbor—a small man, baldheaded, with a long nose and a scraggly mustache above a receding chin. His darting black eyes didn't miss much, and he regarded himself as a source of information for almost anything you might mention. Nothing gave him greater pleasure than to be the bearer of news.

He took off his battered hat and mopped his face and head with a red handkerchief. He didn't have his "store teeth" in as usual, and tobacco stained the corners of his mouth.

"Hello, Joe," he said. He'd told Father long ago not to expect him to call him Reverend. He didn't believe in church nonsense, and as far as he was concerned, Father was just plain Joe O'Neill.

"Hear the news?" He gummed his tobacco excitedly and didn't wait for Father to answer. "That sheepherder over the hill got hisself killed last night. Wonder you didn't see the light of the fire. Sheep wagon almost burned up. There was a shootin' first, though. Sykes folks went over when they seen the blaze, and they seen another fellow hightailin' it out of there. That half-burned young fellow had a hole clean through his head. They think they was drinkin' and fightin' over cards."

"My word! We weren't aware of a thing! As much as he irritated us with his sheep, I couldn't wish such a horrible thing to happen. I didn't blame him, anyway. He was just a tool of Cavinder."

Father could talk this way in front of Dad Jahns because the old man had his own troubles with Cavinder.

"From all I heard, that young feller was just sheepherding for his health. He had TB. Well, he's cured now, that ain't no joke."

Father didn't crack a smile at that. Just shook his head in sympathy.

"I hear Cavinder's going to go in for cattle. Shipped in three carloads of longhorns and turned 'em loose north of Provo on government land," Dad Jahns said.

"Do you mean he is going to give up sheep raising?"

"No, guess he's going to have both. If he can't keep the range one way, he'll keep it another."

Chapter 11

The Longhorns

I've heard of people having to clean their floors with a hoe in the old days, but I never thought I'd be doing it," Mother said as she attacked the dried mud in the lean-to kitchen. "Bring me half a pail of water from the rain barrel, Lenna, and Verna, you bring me the scrub brush, please."

Father had set out that morning on the two-day trip to Hot Springs to apply for citizenship. He was accompanied by James Sykes and Art Bartlett, who went along to swear that he had lived in the county two years or more. Mother planned to clean and organize the house while he was gone. She never gave in to the prairie dust and dirt that found its way into our little house. She kept it as clean as our town house had ever been. "You girls go out and play while I finish this up," she said, shooing us out of her way.

The spring day was balmy without the customary wind that dried the soil and wore nerves thin. Pastel flowers on sunny hillsides gave a blue tone to the greening land as far as the eye could see. Fragrant sagebrush along the crest of the uplands flaunted a deeper purple than usual against the clean, blue sky. Water from melted winter snow stood high in the water holes along the valley. When we came to the draw, I looked to see if the blackbird's nest still clung to the wild rose branches overhanging the water. Father had showed it to me one afternoon when he and I were walking the fields as we often did on Sunday afternoons. I couldn't see the nest anywhere and wondered if the blackbird bowing to us from the cattails was the same one that had spread its red-patched wings and scolded us away from her mottled blue eggs.

Verna and I wandered farther from the house than we ever had. We didn't return with our handfuls of flowers for Mother until nearly noon. She had finished cleaning the house and had washed her long, dark-brown hair. Still damp, it hung all the way down to her hips, and a bright ribbon held it back from her face.

"May I brush your hair this time?" I asked. Verna and I loved to comb and arrange Mother's hair, and although she had to struggle with the snarls later, she sometimes permitted us to do this while she read stories aloud to us.

"I think it's Verna's turn," Mother said, and though I pleaded that I had asked first, Verna became the hairdresser. I was cross, and after lunch decided to do something else instead of listen to Mother's reading.

Mother had to sit in a straight-backed chair so Verna could reach to comb out the tangles. I settled myself facing the window in the rocking chair, my back turned to Mother and Verna to broadcast my bad temper. Queen exhaled an occasional whimper, deep in dreams beneath the table. A lazy breeze stirred the strip of fly paper hanging from the ceiling. My eyes felt heavy in the afternoon heat. I rested my feet on the window sill and cut out paper dolls. Only Mother's droning voice interrupted the stillness as she read the story from *The Youth's Companion*.

In the blink of an eye, darkness replaced the golden light. Instead of blue sky and green prairie, I faced two bulging, unblinking eyes peering through the open window. I froze. The long face of the hairy giant nudged against the sill. Its pointed ears drew back. We stared at each other. Neither of us blinked. I didn't even breathe. Queen's hysterical barking broke the spell, and the creature snorted and lifted its massive head.

"Mother!" I tumbled backward and overturned the chair.

"For goodness sakes, Lenna," she scolded until she saw the beast and stared open-mouthed before she jumped up, slammed the door shut, and turned the lock. Queen kept up her protective barking. I gripped the overturned rocker in fear. Verna stayed rooted to her post behind the chair, the brush in her frozen, raised hand.

"We're surrounded by Texas longhorns!" Mother cried. "The gate's open! More are coming in!"

The cattle with sharp-pointed horns three or four feet long poured in, so many we couldn't count them, even if we'd had the courage to go out and try. Unlike the sheep that had taken fright at any sound we made, the cattle were curious and belligerent. They stood their ground and snorted at Queen when Mother pushed her onto the front stoop. Their horns raked the sides of the house as they vied with each other to lean against the corners and scratch their leathery hides. Their massive bodies shook the room, and their snouts poked in the windows and terrified us.

Mother kept on reading to us. "They'll go away. There must be someone who will come looking for them. Now don't worry. We're quite safe. We'll just pretend they're not there."

Pretense ended with a particularly shattering blow against the house. One steer had bunted another into the wall. The dishes in the corner cupboard began toppling to the floor from the box shelves improvised by Father.

"My wedding dishes!" Mother tried to catch them, but they shattered all around her. "No, no, no!"

When the last dish smashed on the floor, Mother slumped down on the rocker. Tears streamed down her cheeks. Verna and I had seldom seen Mother cry. We stared at her for a moment, and then started in too.

"It's all right, girls. Don't cry. I shouldn't either, but I liked the dishes so much. Now they're gone." She dried her cheeks on her apron. "They belonged to another sort of life," she whispered. Then she rearranged herself and straightened her back. "That fragile china wouldn't do very well for us out here on the homestead anyway."

We swept up Mother's flowery white dishes and collected the pieces in the coal scuttle. Mother wound up her hair and pinned it high on her head. I picked up the paper dolls, but my joy in them was gone, and I tried to listen carefully as Mother began to read aloud again.

By late afternoon, the cattle had wandered off. They drifted east onto government land. A horseman rounded up the herd and drove it on over the ridge. Mother inspected the gate and found that the wire loop that held the gate shut had been broken. She tied a rope to replace it and came in the house to get supper ready.

That night, the yapping and howling of the coyotes sounded very near our small prairie home. Although these sounds were growing more familiar, it comforted us to have Queen with us, though she'd slept when she should have been warning us of the longhorn invasion. Mother blew out the lamp earlier than usual, but we all lay awake for a long time listening to the rain patter on the roof. Father had only been gone one day, but without him out on the dark prairie, scared witless by the monster cows, we missed him.

Chapter 12

The Baptism

Father never lost sight of his primary mission to bring the word of the Lord into the Wild West and to serve his congregations. However, when Mr. Coleman insisted on an immersion baptism, Father dug in his heels.

Mr. Coleman kept pressing, and Father kept putting him off. While the physical aspects of baptism were not that important to Father, he was disturbed by Mr. Coleman's stubborn refusal to have anything but immersion. The dry prairies had no Jordan River and no baptismal large enough for the likes of the tall, barrel-chested homesteader. Plus, his insistence on immersion irked Father's sense of Christian submission, but he could not convince Mr. Coleman to settle for the usual touching of water to the brow. He told Father he'd been raised a Baptist and knew his Bible. The only genuine baptism, according to Mr. Coleman, was by immersion.

Late in the summer, Mr. Coleman stopped by our place on his way to the Sykes place for some pigs he had bought. He didn't stay long, but by the time he left, it had been decided he would be immersed in his windmill tank. The baptism would take place a week from Sunday in a private ceremony for close friends and family.

"Now, that's what I call practical," said Mother with a twinkle in her eyes. "You can go to the house afterward and get your wet clothes off in a hurry." She was, as usual, thinking about Father's health.

Father wasn't too pleased with the plan. "I shouldn't say it, I suppose, but I hope they scrub up that tank a bit for the ceremony."

"I just hope it's a hot day so you won't get chilled," Mother said.

Father still suffered a persistent hacking cough, though his health had already improved in the few, short months we'd been in Provo. "Nonsense," he said. "I don't expect the water will be above my knees. If it's a sweltering day like today, it will be a pleasure to stand in the cool water."

A fierce sun beat down on us the afternoon of the baptism, and a stiff, scorching wind whipped across the dry prairies as Father guided the Model T along the ruts west of Provo. Father hadn't slept well the night before, and Mother had insisted on his trying to take a little nap after lunch. Now we were almost late.

Father drove faster than usual down the deserted main street of Provo. The dust blew into a long plume behind us, and we hung onto our hats as Father gathered extra speed to climb the last hill. At the summit, we stared in amazement at the jumble of wagons, teams, buggies, and riding horses gathered in the Colemans' yard.

Father tightened his grip on the steering wheel and muttered something about "a regular circus." He drove down and parked beside a lumber wagon. After pulling the emergency brake, he gave the motor a little extra gas and leaned down to turn off the engine at the magneto box. A crack like gunfire turned all heads toward us. Even the children chasing each other around the fringes of the crowd heard the *pop, pop, pop* of the backfiring engine. Everyone stopped to stare as the O'Neills got out of their car, late for the baptism.

Even when facing a crowd of bemused onlookers, Father's natural dignity and good manners prevailed. He handed Mother down with his usual old-world gallantry. I handed him the suitcase containing his change of clothes and his leather satchel, and he strode off toward the squat, rambling house. Mother caught up with him as he mingled with the waiting crowd and laughed at the sallies of "Arriving with a bang," "Free advertising," and so on.

I had never been so close to a windmill before and was astounded at its height. The wind wheel flapped and whirred, and the swinging arm groaned and screeched. I tiptoed and peered over the edge to watch the water rush out of the rusty pipe into the large, round, wooden tank. I knew Father would be disappointed over the green moss and scum that clung to the boards. The brown, murky water smelled fresh and cool and made a lovely music as it ran out of the pipe. My fingers floated lazily in the rippling water until I heard a woman say something about "the preacher's daughter." The memory of the angry mothers back in Edgemont who'd accused me of saying naughty things lingered. I took off running and ended up down by the barn.

Around the corner, some of the children were paying rapt attention to Ivan Humphrey, who normally didn't have much to say. His folks rarely came to church because Mr. Humphrey had a big puckered hole in one cheek where a cancer had been cut out. It was hard not to stare at his scarred face the few times I had seen him.

"Right there is where that bronc ran right up the side of the stack and out onto the roof of the shed," he was saying. "Broke his neck when he fell off into the corral. Good horse too. Guess the south pasture is plumb full of loco weed. Coleman's ain't runnin' their horses—"

Chris Coleman ran up and cut him off. "Quiet! C'mon over by the tank. Ma says the baptism is beginning."

Everyone had gathered around the windmill. Father and Mr. Coleman stood near the tank. We children scattered to be with our parents, and when we all quieted down, Father said, "Let us bow our heads in prayer." As he said the prayer, I heard the sounds around us. The windmill squeaked above us. A meadowlark sang its liquid song. A hen cackled over by the chicken house. The horses stomped and swished their tails to swat the flies. The cottonwood leaves rattled. Above it all, Father's rolling Irish brogue brought us all to the presence of God. I forgot about the dust, the flies, and the smell of the barnyard. "Amen," Mr. Coleman said, and others followed suit.

Father said a few words and read a verse, then handed his Bible to Mother. Mr. Coleman pulled off his shoes and stepped onto a wooden box that was supposed to make it easier to climb over the edge of the tank. He swung himself over the edge and tumbled into the water, splashing everybody by the tank, including Father. Father kept the oxfords on that he'd fished out of the missionary box especially for the occasion. He'd said he didn't mind ruining them since he didn't like them in the first place. Straddling the tank edge precariously with his legs all akimbo to balance himself, he slid in. Once the waves settled down, the water reached the middle of his thighs.

The water soaked into Mr. Coleman's clean blue overalls and crept up his starched white shirt all the way to his broad, powerful shoulders. A red-striped tie wrapped his thick neck. Standing there with his arms folded and the sun glinting off his bald head, he looked like a giant.

Father looked small beside Mr. Coleman. He was almost as tall but much thinner. He had put on his good suit coat and a white shirt and tie, but he had changed his pants. Mother and Father had argued about this. The extra pants were old and didn't matter, but father had just one good suit coat. Mother was afraid it might be ruined, but father had been adamant. He must look like a minister, he said, water or no water. It would be expected, and he would not disappoint the people. Besides, he would feel better properly dressed.

"You're always telling me to avoid getting chilled. If for no other reason, that's why I need to wear the coat." That had ended the discussion.

Father said another prayer standing with his face lifted toward the sky, his hands clasped a few inches above the water lapping at his legs. Then he turned and took Mr. Coleman's hand and the big man knelt down in the water. Father put his hands on Mr. Coleman's shoulders and tipped him forward until he was completely under.

"I baptize thee in the name of the Father, the Son, and the Holy Ghost."

Mr. Coleman emerged red-faced, holding his nose. Water poured off him in great rivers. He spread his arms, threw back his head and exclaimed, "Praise the Lord! I'm born again!"

The crowd hushed, and the only sounds were the dripping water and the screeching of the windmill. Father began to sing in his fine baritone: "Praise God from whom all blessings flow. Praise Him all creatures here below," and before he had finished the first few words, the people were singing with him.

The water gushed out of Father's shoes when he stepped out of the tank, and I could hear him sloshing all the way to the house. But he was right, the coat, except for one front corner, was as pressed and dry and proper as could be.

Mr. Coleman walked around in his wet clothes, his face shining with happiness. "Come on in. Ma has fixed egg salad and sardine sandwiches and lemonade." He shook hands with everyone and tried to hug a few, but they didn't want any part of getting wet.

Before going inside, some of the men stooped to drink from the windmill pipe, and we children lined up behind them. Though I was only six, I'd already lived in that parched country long enough to understand that Mr. Coleman had been washed in God's most precious earthly treasure. When it came my turn, I leaned over that murky tank and drank deep.

Chapter 13

Back to Edgemont

Verna and Lenna O'Neill holding puppies

Mother leaned way out the window of the Model T and exclaimed, "There's an Indian village behind our house!" It was September 1915. The car was loaded to the top. We were moving back to Edgemont for the winter after satisfying the six-month residency on the homestead.

Our new home was a small house at the edge of town, not the parsonage, which was rented out to a railroad family. When we pulled up in front, we saw a sea of white tents in an open field behind the house. Mother's voice rose to a squeal. "There must be a hundred of them."

"My word! I heard the Lakota would come down from the Pine Ridge Reservation for the fair, but I didn't dream there'd be so many," Father said, "or that they would be camped here, for goodness sake."

Before we could even step out of the car, Mother turned in her seat and said, "You girls are not to leave the house without Papa or me. And Queen is not to go outside either. Do you understand?" She sounded so agitated I thought she might make us stay in the car for the whole time the Indians were in town.

"There's nothing to be afraid of," Father said. "If they were dangerous, they wouldn't be here." He didn't sound so calm either.

A stack of quilts and pillows in her arms muffled Mother's reply. "Well, it's better to be safe than sorry."

As we helped carry things in, Verna said, "Mother didn't count very well. There are only twenty-six tents."

I kept walking as I peeked over the box I was carrying. I wasn't nearly as enthusiastic about the Indian village as Verna. Out of the corner of my eye, I saw tents arranged in a circle and lots of wagons—prairie schooners, lumber wagons, spring wagons—lined up beside them. Other than some tethered horses, I didn't see any signs of life.

"Where are the Indians? Why don't we see any Indians?" Verna said. She was so excited she forgot about helping to unload. Instead, she stood with her hand shielding her eyes from the sun, surveying the scene.

"They're probably all at the fair," Father said. "Come on, now. You'll see them later on."

We went inside and inspected our new home, which came furnished. Verna and I set to work spreading featherbeds, unpacking dishes, and arranging the cupboards. Mother hung curtains at the windows, and we helped her put away clothes in an armoire and dressers. Meanwhile, Father discovered that the pitcher pump in the kitchen didn't work. He went downtown for new leathers to fix it.

By late afternoon, we'd finished moving in, and that freed us up to watch the Indian village from our window. An Indian woman came out of a tent and built a fire in front of it, then brought a kettle and hung it over the flames. Verna's nose was pressed against the glass, but I hung back. The woman looked familiar to me.

"Could that Indian lady be the same one who tried to steal our puppies in Ree Heights that time?" I said.

Mother glanced out the window. "Oh, no. These aren't the same Indians at all, Lenna. They come from a different reservation entirely."

I knew she must be right, but I kept a careful eye on that woman. I had reason to be wary. My upper lip bore a scar that resulted from an encounter with a transient Indian woman several years before. She had leaned over the fence and called softly to Queen's puppies playing in the yard. Though I was only four years old, I dashed from the house to save them. I heard stories about Indians making dog soup, and I was terrified she would take Queen or one of the pups. I tripped, and my mouth landed on a nail sticking up from a loose board. Bloodied but unbowed, I scooped up the three puppies and raced into the house with Queenie in tow. My finger rubbed over the bumpy ridge of the scar, and a shudder raced through me.

Still, I found it hard to walk away from the window. After awhile, an Indian man driving a team and wagon arrived at the tents, followed by more Indians in wagons, riders on ponies, and men and women on foot. I had never seen anything so exotic.

From our safe perch, we watched the camp come alive. Before long, fires burned in pits in front of the tents. The horses were hobbled or tethered and put out to graze. Dogs ran alongside children snaking and darting through campsites past women preparing meals and clusters of men talking and laughing. Their voices were muted, but the barking of the dogs rung out loud and clear. Father wasn't going to like that, I thought.

"What is that hanging between those poles near that tepee?" I asked Mother. She pulled back the curtain and followed my gaze.

"It looks like strips of meat," she said. "I'll bet she's making jerky. Probably has more than she needs for the meal and is drying the rest. That will cure fast enough in this dry wind."

Father came back with the leathers and joined us at the window. "With this heat, I hope we don't get a whiff of that meat day after tomorrow. Whew! And think of the flies!"

Father set to work fixing the pump and told us what he'd learned in town about the Indians. Apparently, they came to Edgemont each year to participate in the fair, doing their dances and riding their ponies and such.

"You'll never believe the chief's name," Father said. "Chief Stinking Bear." We all laughed. "He's quite a man, I'm told. He sent his daughter to an Eastern school, yet he's the most traditional Indian of the whole tribe." Verna and I couldn't stop giggling over his name.

"By the way," Father said, "there's an Indian dance and barbeque downtown tonight. Wish we could go, but I don't suppose the preacher should be seen at such an exhibition."

"I don't know why not," Mother protested. "I want to go, and I think the girls should go. It will be one of those times they'll never forget." I did want to see it, but I couldn't get that Indian woman out of my head. Verna jumped up and down with glee, but I nibbled at the scar on my lip and tried not to think about her anymore.

Walking down the dusty road toward Main Street, we found ourselves in the midst of the Indians heading downtown. None of them paid any attention to us, but I clung to Father's hand and shivered a little. Verna and Mother walked close behind us. A young man in front of us trailed a long feather from a ponytail on top of his head. He was bare from the waist up except for beaded bands on his forearms and feather cuffs at his wrists. He carried a wing fan and a gourd rattle, which he shook gently in rhythm with his steps. The others near us talked and laughed quietly, but this young man didn't say a word.

At the center of town, a crowd gathered around Indians standing in a circle at the crossroads. We could smell the beef roasting above the hot coals in the pit at the side of the street.

"Can't we get in a little closer so the girls can see?" whispered Mother.

Father placed me in front of him, and before I realized what he was doing, I was standing with my shoulder pressed hard against the metal horse-watering trough in front of White's Store. Then Verna emerged from the crowd to stand beside me. We could see Mother and Father but couldn't touch them.

The dance began with the pounding of a drum. A blue-painted, near-naked brave danced toward us, his feet padding silently in the dust of the road, his steps as quick and light as the feathers tied to his ankles. He came toward us, danced back, and then came toward us again. He leaned backward and shook a feathered wand against the sky. Bending and swaying, his body moved in rhythm with the insistent drumbeats. He passed so near we could have touched him, but his eyes focused on something far, far away. We heard the people around us murmur his name—Blue Eagle. He whirled and leaped and bent low but never slowed his lightning steps. There was no mistaking that this was a war dance, threatening, proud, joyful, and wild.

Some of the younger Indian boys tried dancing with Blue Eagle and the other men, but the women and smaller children remained at the outer edge of the circle, moving almost imperceptibly sideways, gliding their feet, then gracefully dipping at the knees in perfect time with the beat of the tom-toms. Their eyes stayed fixed on the men in the ring. The old women looked almost too frail to bear the weight of rows of elk teeth on the yokes of their deerskin dresses. The young women wore bright, printed gathered skirts. Strands of colored beads hung from their necks and swayed with their delicate movements. They chanted the eerie, high-pitched song along with the drummers and dancers in the ring.

During an intermission, a white man passed a hat through the crowd taking a collection for the dancers. Soon there was a loud drumbeat, a rhythm started, a singer began the plaintive chant, and the dance began again.

Blue Eagle, the drummers, and the serious, graceful women moving to the strange music that beat like my heart enthralled and confused me. I'd been taught to fear the Indians, and yet, what I'd seen was dignified and beautiful. "Let's go home," I said.

"Oh, no, not yet," cried Verna.

Father and Mother agreed, and Verna dawdled, hanging back just a bit as we walked and talked quietly about the extraordinary night. The fires of the Indian camp burned brightly beyond our house. Tom-toms pounded a slow and steady beat. A high, thin wail rose above the mournful sound.

The music continued long after we were all in bed. Father tossed in his bed and grumbled, "It sounds like a dirge."

"That singing went on all night. Papa couldn't sleep a wink," Mother said when she called us the next morning. "He's still in bed. I'm going to go down to Stalford's to see what I can find out."

She was back before we left the breakfast table. "Girls, I'll have to wake your father. The chief's daughter, the one he sent away to college, has died. All the Indians are mourning, and that's the sound we've been hearing. Mrs. Stalford says the message came by telegraph last night while the dance was going on. Oh, I feel so sorry for him."

I remembered when Verna was so sick with the whooping cough and how scared I was that she would die. "Why did she have to die?" I asked, following her to the bedroom.

"She had appendicitis, they say," Mother said. "Joe, you'll have to get up." Mother sat down on the bed and gently jostled Father. "Chief Stinking Bear's daughter is dead. That's what the chanting was about."

"Oh, my. That explains the mournful sound. So much like our own funeral music, wasn't it?"

Mother nodded and gave him a gentle tug. "Don't you think you should go over there and help that poor man in his sorrow?"

"I wonder if we could understand each other." Though he looked skeptical, Father got up and came out to the kitchen. "Poor man. I don't suppose he's a Christian," he said.

Mother ladled oatmeal into a bowl and poured a cup of coffee. "He's a sorrowing human, and it's our place to comfort him if we can." Father ate hurriedly and gulped some coffee. He put on his white collar and his black jacket, and with his Bible tucked under his arm, he walked out the door.

When Father told us about his condolence visit with the chief, the last of my fear of the Indians dropped away. He told us how sorrowful the chief was and how everyone in the tent village had gathered around him, just like we did at our funerals. I guessed they felt just as bad as we did at those times when we lost one of our own.

The next morning, I thought I might venture close enough to the Indian village to catch sight of Blue Eagle or the chief. As soon as I stepped outside, I saw there was nothing but a pile of tin cans, some paper flying about, and black circles of dead campfires. The Indians had vanished during the night.

Chapter 14

Roy is Born

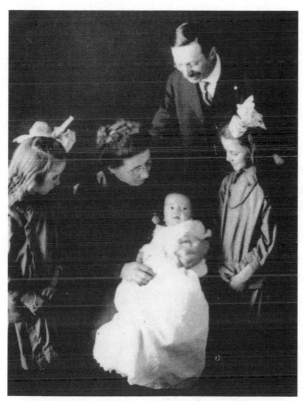

(left to right) Verna O'Neill, Dora O'Neill,
Joseph O'Neill, and Lenna O'Neill with
baby Roy O'Neill

Before dawn on a frozen November morning, Father was organizing his gear for a deer-hunting trip with Hubert Bartlett. A light snow had fallen the afternoon before that made for perfect tracking conditions. But once the Model T was packed and Father was ready to go, he hesitated. "I wonder if I really ought to go, Dearie. Are you sure you will be all right?"

I wondered why Mother, who'd taken care of us and the house plenty of times while Father was gone, would not be all right without him this time. Just like I expected, she waved him off, reassuring him that she'd be fine.

It was laundry day, and the morning sped by. We girls carried water for Mother to boil the clothes in the big copper pot. The house filled with steam, and we soon forgot the chilly morning as we wiped the sweat from our brows. Mother transferred the laundry to the tub of the wooden washing machine and Verna and I took turns pulling the handle back and forth to run the agitator. When it was time to hang the clothes on the line in the backyard, we handed her the pins and shook out the wrinkles. The sheets froze solid almost as soon as they were hung. They made a wonderful cracking sound when we sneaked by and gave them a whack.

By noon, Mother seemed unusually tired and cross, and I was delighted when she sent me down to Stalford's.

"Mamma says she isn't feeling very well and wonders if Mrs. Stalford will come over for awhile," I said to Elsie when she came to the door. To my surprise, both Elsie and her mother put on their coats and accompanied me back to the house.

As soon as we got back, Elsie said to Verna and me, "Come on, let's go for a walk." She was several years older than we were and often stayed with us when both Mother and Father had to be gone. We weren't used to having her as a playmate, so we felt flattered and hustled into our play clothes.

She walked with us up to the reservoir on the hill. The big wooden tank stored water from the artesian well, pumped up there to cool and supply Edgemont with the first decent drinking water it ever had. We romped for awhile with Queen before we sat with our backs to the water tank, out of the icy wind.

"Mother says we're going to have a big surprise for Christmas, Elsie, and we can't think what it can be," Verna said, breathless with excitement.

I whistled for Queen, pretending to ignore Verna's chatter. I liked to keep things to myself, but Verna could never resist blurting everything that was on her mind.

"I know what the surprise is, but I can't tell you," Elsie said, teasing us.

This got my attention. The surprise must be really big if others knew about it besides Mother and Father. We begged Elsie to tell us, but she wouldn't budge.

Finally, we gave up and went back down to the house. That night, in our bed, Verna and I talked long about what our surprise could possibly be.

"It has to be the riding pony," I said.

"I hope it will be black."

"With a long mane and tail."

"Maybe with a white face?"

"No, all black and shiny," I insisted.

We were about to drop off to sleep when there was a shuffling of feet in the front room. "I just couldn't stay away overnight, Dearie," Father said. "I knew I wouldn't sleep for thinking about you. The snow is too deep up there in the hills anyway. The going's too hard. We saw tracks but couldn't get a shot. We decided we might as well come on home."

I wondered again at Father's unusual concern over Mother, though it was true she did have a backache all day, and she had asked me to get Mrs. Stalford, who'd stayed for supper and was still here. Was Mother sick and not telling us?

I woke the next morning to the sound of Mrs. Stalford's cheery voice. "Well! You girls going to sleep all day?" She looked down on us, her fists on her broad hips. "Get up and get dressed and see what a wonderful surprise you have."

We fumbled with our clothes and rushed through washing our faces at the sink. The horse! The horse! Our black pony had arrived!

Then doubt crept in. It wasn't Christmas, so why were we being awakened so early? And why was Mrs. Stalford still here? Where was Mother? Father?

"Your breakfast can wait. Come let's see the surprise," Mrs. Stalford said as she ushered us into Mother and Father's bedroom.

The window shade had been pulled against the bright morning sun. Father stood next to the bed, but it took a few seconds for my eyes to adjust before I saw Mother under the quilts, propped up against a pile of pillows.

"Come see what a wonderful surprise we have for you, girls," Mother said. "Can you guess what it is?" Her voice was so happy it almost sounded like singing.

I hesitated, but Verna said, "Is it our black pony?"

Father and Mrs. Stalford laughed. Mother smiled and said, "It's much nicer than that. Look here."

I sensed Verna fidgeting next to me, but neither of us took our eyes off Mother in the bed. My mind raced. It could not possibly be the pony. But what? What? She lifted the quilt away from her shoulder, and I felt my whole body deflate, like a high-flying kite diving out of the sky. There, nestled in the crook of her arm, lay a red, wrinkled baby.

"You have a baby brother," she said.

I was speechless, and for once, so was Verna. This was something we hadn't thought about at all. What was so wonderful about having a baby brother? Both Mother and Father had agreed we should have a pony when we returned to the claim in the spring. We had talked all fall about the pony, but instead here was a baby.

"A baby brother is what Papa and I wanted most in all the world for you girls," Mother said. "And our prayers have been answered. We're so happy, and we know you will be too."

Father sat down next to Mother and patted her arm. I thought she might cry, but she was still smiling.

"Come on girls," Mrs. Stalford said. "Let's have some breakfast. When the baby wakes up, we'll let you get better acquainted."

Father came out and sat down to breakfast with us. Verna and I were miserable with disappointment. We watched numbly as Father took his napkin out of his silver napkin ring. Clearly, he'd known all along we were getting a brother instead of a pony.

"I'm surely glad I came home from that hunting trip. I wasn't home an hour when I had to get Dr. Thompson," Father said.

"You have a fine, healthy boy there. Everything went well, and that's something to be grateful for," Mrs. Stalford said.

"Your brother will ride that pony with you girls one day. You wait and see," Father said.

Verna and I looked at each other and reflected a small hint of relief. A brother wouldn't be so bad if we were going to have the pony too!

Verna broke the silence we'd maintained since first laying eyes on that baby. "What's his name?"

Grandma arrived three days later and stayed with us until after Christmas. We loved having her with us. She was happy and lively and went about the house singing. She told us funny stories and taught us how to do embroidery stitches. This visit was different, though, because the baby took so much of her time, as well as Mother's. We felt left out.

Mother and Grandma talked nonstop as they cooked and cleaned and cared for the new baby, whose name we found out that first morning when Verna finally asked was Roy. As they boiled the laundry one afternoon, Grandma brought up the same subject she'd been harping on since she'd arrived. She was not at all sure we should return to the homestead, especially now that there was a baby. "Central South Dakota is bad enough. Why did you have to settle out here in this godforsaken land?" she demanded to know.

Grandma did the heavy lifting while Mother worked the agitator on the machine. "We've decided it is the right thing for us, Mother. Joe's health is improving. The doctor says outdoor work and sun are what he needs, and it seems God has given us this opportunity to help him get well and earn some security for ourselves at the same time." The two of them stood over the tub, looking down at the swirling white diapers. "We know it will be hard, but you can't talk us out of it. Wait till you see the claim. Maybe you'll feel different."

"Well, now I know I'm right," Grandma said the moment she came in the door. In an attempt to dispel her fears, Father had taken Grandma out to the homestead in the Model T. "Not only is that a desert out there, but it's filled with wild beasts!"

"What in the world—" Mother said.

"A wolf attacked the car, that's what," Grandma exclaimed. "Ask Joe."

Father hung his coat in the closet and turned to Mother, blowing on his cold hands. "If it hadn't happened to me, I'd hardly believe it myself. We were in those deep ruts just before you get to the Roberts' place, and there in front of us were three coyotes. For awhile, they ran ahead of us. Then the two smaller ones took off to the left, but the one kept on ahead of us. It jumped to the higher ground, and I thought we were rid of it. Instead, it turned and lunged at us as we went by."

Mother gasped. Verna's eyes widened to saucers. I was dumbfounded.

"Of course, there was no real danger to us, but it was a vicious-looking beast," Father added.

"It was on my side of the car, right beside my door. Right beside me," Grandma said, making the point with her thick fingers thumping the kitchen table. "If it hadn't been for the side curtains, it could have struck me."

"What do you suppose, Joe? I never heard of a coyote doing such a thing. Do you suppose it thought it was fighting for its life?"

"I have no idea, but it was bigger than the usual coyote, and grayer. It rose upon its hind legs, which made it look even more fierce. I'll admit it gave us both a fright. I was glad I wasn't driving the team."

"Maybe it was loco," Mother said.

"Far as I know, coyotes don't eat loco weeds," Father said. "Besides, there are no weeds to eat this time of year."

"There's been talk about a killer timber wolf in the foothills of the Black Hills," Mother said. "Could he have come down this far?"

"Timber wolves or coyotes, you couldn't hire me to live out there, and I might as well say it right out. I think you're making a terrible mistake planning to move back this spring. There isn't room for three children and you two in that tiny shack of a house anyway," Grandma said.

"Shh. You'll wake the baby," Mother said.

"I imagine it won't get much sleep with all of you underfoot in that house," Grandma said.

"We'll make the house bigger, and we won't be so isolated. Telephones are going to be put in all down the valley this spring," Mother said, sounding much calmer after her initial fright.

"Everything looked fine at the claim," Father said. "On the way back, there were no coyotes or wolves or any dangerous beasts, just jackrabbits. The prairie is full of them. Wish I'd taken my gun. We'd have had rabbit for supper." He clapped his hands together and said, "Let's eat. I'm starving." That was the last we ever heard from Grandma on the subject.

Chapter 15

Moving the Shack

O ne of those dad-blamed critters caught me square,"
Grandpa exclaimed. He stormed across the yard at our
little house in Provo. "I'm going back with a gun and some
traps and make fur pelts out of those gol-darned critters!"

Grandpa had come out from Ree Heights to help Father
move an abandoned shack from an adjacent claim. He'd been
working alone that day, jacking up the one-room, tar-papered
house. He and Father planned on setting wheels under it and
hauling it to our yard. Unfortunately he had not anticipated
one problem. A family of skunks lived under the house and
resisted eviction. Our first knowledge of this circumstance was
the noxious odor that preceded him as he approached the
house.

"Don't come into the house," Mother screamed, holding
her nose. "Stay there! Stay there! I'll get you some clean
clothes."

Grandpa changed his clothes in the barn, but he still
stunk. Mother would not let him come into the house.

"You'll have to take a bath," she said. "Wash your hair too."

Mother showed him the galvanized wash tub hanging
outside the house. She ladled all the hot water out of the stove

reservoir into pails and handed them out the door to Grandpa, along with some lye soap. We heard him in the barn scolding himself as he scrubbed away the terrible smell. He threw all his original clothes in the wash water and took the scrub brush to them too.

He came out of the barn, carrying the wet clothes and still muttering. "Dad-burned critters. I'll teach you. No more traps. Going to use a gun."

"Dad, you simply can't come in the house smelling like that," said Mother.

"It's not me, it's these wet clothes."

"Well, you can't put those smelly things on my clothesline!"

Grandpa glared at Mother briefly, turned around, and went back to the barn. Shortly afterwards, he came out with a spade, as well as the wet clothes. He stomped to the pasture, dug a hole, dropped the wet clothes in, and pounded the dirt back into the hole with the back of the spade.

"Better use the scrub brush on those shoes," called Mother when he came back.

It was days before Grandpa's fragrant shoes didn't advertise his presence wherever he went. The skunk family held up the house moving the better part of two days, but Grandpa shot it out with them, and had five pelts stretched on the side of the barn for his trouble. On his insistence, Mother accepted one of the carefully dressed-out skunks. She slow roasted it to extract as much of the fat as possible. The odorless oil she obtained served as the base of our main cold remedy. She mixed it with camphor gum dissolved in alcohol and rubbed it on our chests at the first sign of a cold.

On house-moving day, Father borrowed Jim Bushnell's tractor and hooked it on to the house. Grandpa walked alongside, and Verna and I rode in the house on wheels. We ran from one window to the other and waved gaily at Grandpa. An old calendar swung back and forth on the wall as the flat-rimmed wheels ground slowly down the lane. The painted scene on the tin stopper in the stovepipe depicted woods and a stream and an Indian maid paddling a birchbark canoe. When a sudden lurch sent us skidding across the floor, we sat down and pretended to be Indian princesses navigating rough waters.

Before we knew it, Grandpa swung open the door. "Get out girls, and go to the house. It's going to take some doing to maneuver this through the fence and up against the house. We can't be worrying about you too."

Father and Grandpa managed to get it situated next to the north side of the house, creating an L-shape. Before Grandpa went home, he helped build a lean-to in the elbow of the L. That gave us four rooms—the homestead house with its added lean-to kitchen and the new building with a lean-to bedroom.

Mother set to work plastering the walls using pasted newspaper and cloth, and in a short time, there was wallpaper and lace curtains at the windows. Grandpa and Father moved the rest of our furniture from Edgemont. At last we had a real home in Provo, big enough for all of us.

Chapter 16

Duke

When Grandpa left and all the hard work was done, Father's health declined again. He'd lost weight, and he seemed more nervous. I often awoke to hear him coughing during the night. Years later, Mother confided that Dr. Thompson had told her, "His only hope is to get outdoors into the sun, and completely away from the strain of public work. At that, he may not win. It is only fair to tell you."

At the end of April, Father gave notice to his churches that he would give up his ministry on the first of July. He borrowed the machinery to plant crops, and the bank loaned him the money to buy seed, a team of old mares, and a milk cow. The change did him good. He was happy and content in this new life. There was a lot to learn about farming, and he wasn't able to accomplish as much in a day as his neighbors, but he learned quickly and did all his strength allowed.

We tethered the cow with a long rope on the best grass, and she gave us lots of good-tasting, rich milk. She was an irritable creature though, and we girls always stayed outside the circle of her grazing.

Mr. Sykes saw Father's efforts to make a garden by spading up the sod and came one morning with a walking plow and a team. By noon, we had forty furrows along the north side of the house. Mr. Sykes promised to plow more ground for Father's corn and wheat.

"If the corn is a good crop, maybe I can buy some equipment of my own," Father said. "It's wonderful to have such good neighbors. We're very grateful."

Verna and I helped Father plant the vegetables in long, straight rows. He taught us how to cut up the seed potatoes for planting. Soon we had almost all the garden planted. Mother had told us food prices were high, and we knew we had to raise as much of our food as we could. Always optimistic, Mother planned to sell any surplus.

Though we didn't have much money, Father had bought a fifty-dollar membership in the farmers' cooperative, and we were all glad he did. One of its first projects provided telephones for the members' homes. At last, the isolation of the homesteaders was coming to an end.

In May, after the early planting was done, the telephone line came marching pole by pole over the hills from Provo to our place. Verna and I watched intently as the bright bit of the auger ground through our wall. A wire came through next, and then the telephone man came into the house and attached a wooden telephone to the wall.

We watched in awe as the man turned the small handle. The bell tinkled, and he talked into the strange contraption to someone invisible to us. He taught Mother how to call the others on our line and gave her a card with everyone's distinctive rings. Ours was a long and two shorts.

"To call central, turn the handle," said the man.

"What's central?" Verna asked.

"That's the operator. If you want to call someone not on your line, call her and tell her who you want, and she'll ring them for you."

For days afterwards, Verna and I had fun with imaginary conversations on the telephone. The polished black mouthpiece on its long neck was too high up for us to talk into; to do so, we stood on a chair. We longed to be able to take the receiver off the hook and turn the crank, but that was forbidden. The telephone was a fun game for us, but it was much more serious than that. With the connection to our neighbors and beyond, we no longer felt alone on the prairie.

Father put in many days of work for neighboring farmers in exchange for machinery he borrowed from time to time to do our farm work. Inexperienced as he was, he did his share. The other farmers may have smiled behind their hands when he began to work with them, but he earned their respect.

"There's a new road going in over near Hepner's. Each homesteader is supposed to give a certain number of days work with his team, and he gets paid for it," said Father one day. "I wonder if I could drive someone else's team and earn a little. How I wish I had another horse to use with Molly." The two old mares paid for themselves with the spring work they had done, but one of them died giving birth to a stillborn. This was tragedy for us, but Molly, the surviving mare, had a fine colt.

Father borrowed a horse to work on the road and earned sixty dollars. At the end of the last day of work, he drove into the yard leading a black pony behind the spring wagon. Tired and grimy with road dust, Father called out, "Where are my girls?"

Verna and I raced out of the house, and Father handed each of us a rein.

"Here's your pony, girls."

The black horse with the long, shiny mane and tail took my breath away, but all my excitement stayed locked up inside of me. I feared if I said a word or looked at Verna, our beautiful pony would disappear. We walked around him, stroked his soft coat and his wet nose. The more we touched him, the more real he became. By the time we led him to the barn, we were chattering madly.

"What's his name?" I called.

"When Mr. Hepner sold him to me, he said his boys raced him at the fair last year under the name of Black Prince. That won't do, will it? We'll have to think of a new name."

We'd named Queen's puppy Prince. Hearing his name, he sauntered over from the stoop, wagging his tail.

"No, but it must be a fine name like that," I said.

"We forgot to tell Mother," Verna said. "Mother, Mother, come see! Father brought us a pony!"

Mother appeared in the doorway, drying her hands on her apron. "Such a nice horse," she said, smiling just a little. "What did you have to pay, Joe?"

"Saddle, bridle, and horse cost ninety dollars. I'm sure we got a bargain. Mr. Hepner assured me it's exceptionally gentle, surefooted, swift, and intelligent. Ninety dollars is cheap enough. He even threw in a saddle blanket. I endorsed the check for my work on the road to him. We have only thirty dollars left to pay."

Mother pursed her lips. "We did have to have a riding horse," she said, not sounding entirely convinced. "We'll manage some way."

I'd overheard Mother talking to Grandma about Father. "That man had never even bought himself socks when I first knew him in Chicago. His father bought all the clothes for the family, and Joe never bought anything for himself until he'd worn out what he brought to America with him. Imagine that! He has no business sense because he never had to have any."

The tinge of exasperation was still in her voice when she called us into the house. "Come on, girls. Papa is worn out. Let him put the horses away. Come help get the table set for supper. The pony will be here in the morning."

"Do as Mama says, Verna. Lenna, hold the pony till I get the harnesses off these mares and turn them out for the night. We'll have to get the Cass boys over here one of these days to teach you to ride western style. I can't ride anything but English style, and out here, they think posting is silly."

"What's posting?" I asked.

"I'll show you someday. Now, come on. It's almost dark. The pony is used to being outside, but he'll be all right in the barn for tonight."

He took the saddle out of the back of the spring wagon, and I carried the blanket. The smell of it made me long for tomorrow, when I would ride the pony across the prairie. I pictured myself astride the magnificent beast, looking every bit as regal as the Indian women at the fair.

"Come on, my girl. Let's eat. I'll have to milk that cow by lantern tonight."

Over supper, we tossed out every royal term we knew—Emperor, King, Earl. Father said, "Duke," and we all knew our pony was named.

Chapter 17

The Lamb

In early summer, when the pasque flowers lifted their feathery leaves and the tiny white star crocus carpeted the ground beside them, we began to see sheep again in the tall prairie grass north of us. There were not as many as the year before, but we knew they were Walter Cavinder's.

"He'll never get away with it," Father said. "I'm going to call him on the telephone."

Father met Cavinder quite by chance soon after we moved back to the homestead. He'd gone to the Disbrow General Store in Provo for groceries and was standing by the wagon scale talking to Fred Cass when Cavinder walked up to him.

"Well, Preacher, I hear you've got TB."

Father was so taken aback he didn't say anything.

"That's what my sheepherder had—the one who burned to death in his wagon over your way. Can't lick that stuff, you know. Better go back where you belong. When you decide to go, look me up, and I'll buy your land."

It was the first time Father had been face to face with Cavinder, and he remained speechless for a moment. Then he said, "Sir, are you speaking to me?" Without waiting for a response, he said, "I have nothing to say to you. Good day."

With that, Father turned away from him and entered the store.

Later when he told Mother about it he said, "Why couldn't I have thought of something better to say? That man made me so angry."

"Now, Joe, don't let it upset you. Cavinder's saying you have TB doesn't make it true. He was just trying to scare you. We know it isn't so. He's not going to get our land, and his evil ways will catch up with him someday."

Father cranked the telephone and told the operator to connect him to Cavinder. We heard him ask politely if he realized that his herder was letting the sheep stray onto other people's land. He told us Cavinder had been very courteous, and for awhile, we didn't see any sheep at all.

Then one morning we heard a cacophony of bleating cries and saw a wooly white blanket creeping over the land north of us. Though there were hundreds, the herder was careful to keep the sheep from trespassing on private land.

"They'll ruin the grass," Father said.

"I suppose he has to graze them somewhere," Mother said, "but why so near us?"

Verna and I ran off to play in the wake of the sheep. It was early evening with the sunset's glory still lingering in the sky. We walked down the ruts toward the knobby and stunted fruit trees that surrounded Dad Jahns' tiny brown house. He'd nursed them through the years of drought and wind by carrying water by the pail full from a big water hole nearby. With all his effort, he kept them barely alive, but he never gave up hope that someday he would have fruit from his orchard.

We crossed the wooden culvert below the water hole near our gate, then left the road and walked up an incline to some rocks that jutted out in a shelf. We called this place "town" in our make-believe game. I played Peter to Verna's Louise, the cultured young couple of our imaginations. We walked up to the big rock that was Disbrow's store and gave our order.

"One box of oatmeal, a sack of graham flour, a carton of matches, a can of kerosene, and some rock candy, please," ordered Verna in Louise's lilting British accent.

I pulled my pretend money from my imaginary pants pocket.

With the groceries loaded into our invisible Model T, we began "bzzzzzing" back home. All of a sudden, a small gray creature rose out of the grass and ran haltingly toward us. A weak-legged black-faced lamb stopped a few steps from us, looked at us questioningly, and bleated in a high, quavering voice.

"It must have lost itself from the sheep this morning," I said in wonder. "It's all alone." I reached out a hand, and the lamb nuzzled it.

"Poor little thing. What shall we do?" cried Verna.

Peter and Louise were forgotten as we ran toward home as fast as we could. The wobbly lamb tried to follow. It was so little and bleated so pitifully. We slowed to a walk and let it follow us. Then Verna ran ahead calling to Mother.

"For goodness sake. A lamb," Mother said. "Joe, look here. The girls have found a lamb."

Father appeared behind Mother on the stoop. "My word! Are there other sheep out there, girls? You shouldn't have brought it home. It belongs to Walter Cavinder."

"I know," Verna said. "But it followed us home, and there aren't any other sheep out there at all."

"Well, I'll have to call him and tell him it's here," Father said.

"Oh, can't we keep it? It likes us!" Verna pleaded.

"But it needs its mother. It must have been out there since this morning. It's probably half starved, and it's such a baby," Mother said.

Father went inside and called Cavinder. Verna got down on her knees and hugged the small, restless creature.

Father rejoined us and said, "Cavinder says for us to keep the lamb. He says it must be a bum lamb. The mother probably had twins and didn't realize she was leaving one behind. He said the herders always have a certain number of such orphan lambs that they bottle feed, but that it would be more trouble than it is worth for him to come here and take the lamb to them. He said, 'Let your kids have it for a pet, if you want to bother with it.'"

"Oh, Papa," I cried. Both Verna and I tried to hug the lamb at once.

"I'm warming milk," called Mother from the house. "We'll put some in a baby bottle. Poor little hungry lamb."

That was the only kind thing Walter Cavinder did for us, but we no longer felt so antagonistic toward him. Perhaps Father's honesty and courtesy finally made an impression, or Walter Cavinder finally accepted his changed world. We never knew, but from that day, we were never again bothered by stray sheep. They were on the north range, but they didn't come onto our land. When Cavinder was in the Provo store one day, he gruffly asked Mother how the lamb was doing.

Sammy—named after the resplendent Uncle Sam who pointed his finger at us from the recruiting posters we saw in Edgemont—tagged us about the yard and butted us playfully. By fall, he was a large, husky, young ram. We couldn't bring ourselves to have his tail docked. With his long tail, he always looked a bit ridiculous from the rear.

Sammy spent his days in the company of calves in the pasture closest to the barn and did not know he was a symbol of some sort of peace between the Cavinders and the O'Neills. He was quite another symbol to Minnie Roberts, our neighbor to the west.

The Roberts', brother and sister, spinster and bachelor, had filed on land on the rim of the valley before we had gone on the homestead. Each had a small one-room, flat-roofed, tar-paper-covered shack built across from each other where their claims joined. The ruts that were our road to Edgemont went between these buildings. Their land was poor, but Minnie and Jim plowed the necessary amount of sod, and lived in their shacks the allotted six months of each year waiting out the time until the land was legally theirs.

Jim had a cow, chickens, and a team of horses, but he was a carpenter by trade and was away much of the time building wooden bridges and culverts for the new roads that were gradually tying the prairie communities together.

Minnie was a dressmaker. She spent her lonely free time visiting on the telephone, and she called Mother often. Sometimes she would walk down the ruts to visit us. She was tall, precise, and neat, except for her henna-colored wig, which always looked uncombed, though a hairnet held it firmly, and the small bun on top was pinned with a quantity of brown tortoise-shell hairpins. She did her hand sewing as she and Mother talked. Apparently unable to converse with little girls, she would watch us with interest.

Because Jim was gone so much, she depended on Father to do small chores for her. If sheep or cattle got into the corn-field, it was Father she called. "I declare that woman thinks up things for me to do," he said once, but he always went to her rescue.

When Father built the cave to store root vegetables and home-canned meats, fruits, and vegetables, Mother made the mistake of saying to Minnie, "It will be a place of protection in case of cyclones."

From then on, if the skies looked black and threatening, Minnie scurried down the hill to the shelter of our cave. We seldom went in with her, but she didn't seem to mind. She'd sit on a nail keg and nervously watch the glowering sky through the doorway or close herself in to wait out the roaring hail or pouring rain. Sometimes we didn't know she was there until she emerged after the storm and hurried away, her wig askew as usual, her tall, thin form looking strangely crisp and dry against the drenched land and rain-freshened sky.

When Minnie proved up on her land, she rented a small house in Provo to be more centrally located for her dressmaking business. Before she moved, she came down the road carrying a gift for Mother. It was a pink china plate with deep pink and red roses in the center.

"Now, don't save this for the second wife, Mrs. O'Neill," she said. "You work too hard. And those little girls of yours work too hard too. Never heard of children their age doing chores and cooking the way they do. They'll be old before their time."

"Oh, they play enough. All that energy can be used to help us all, just as well as if they expended it all on play. They learn more this way. Now don't worry about us. We'll miss you, but you're doing the right thing. We'll keep in touch." I could tell by the tone of Mother's voice she was really going to miss Minnie.

Minnie brought along a big wooden candy pail. "Do you folks have some kindling I can borrow? We're out," she said.

"We have corncobs, if they will do," Mother said.

The cobs were in the small pasture where Sammy and the calves were kept. Father had recently turned some young pigs in there too, to separate them from the ones he was fattening for sale. Cobs from the ears of corn he fed them lay all over the ground.

"The girls will pick up the cobs for you, Minnie," Mother said.

"I can do it," Minnie said, closing the gate behind her. She watched the animals warily as she hurried to pick up the cobs.

Sammy evidently thought the fluttering skirt belonged to a member of the family and trotted up to see what was going on. With the wooden pail not quite full, Minnie threw caution to the wind and bent over to get a few more cobs. This was a mistake, as we girls could have told her from experience. Sammy accepted the invitation, backed up a few steps, took aim, and neatly upended Minnie into the cob pail.

Minnie wasn't injured except for her pride and modesty, but the wooden pail was demolished. We girls filled a bushel basket with the cobs and carried it home for her. Sammy, our lamb of peace, went back to munching grass with the calves.

Chapter 18

Getting the Water

Father had been hauling our water by the barrelful from the deep water hole near Dad Jahns' place, but as the shallow water holes dried up in the summer heat, we realized a cistern was an absolute necessity.

Father began digging not far from the lean-to door. For awhile, he could throw out the shovelfuls of dirt, but when he got too deep for this, he rigged up a windlass, and when he signaled, Mother or one of us girls turned the handle and brought up the heavy pail filled with clay. At last the day came when a man from Edgemont helped Father with the cement work. Once the hole was lined with cement, Father built a platform across the top and installed a long-handled pump. To fill the cistern, Father borrowed a team and tank wagon from Mr. Howell and brought load after load from the big water hole. What a wonderful sound the water made when it gushed into the depths, echoing with a high-pitched hollow tone from each tank load.

"Now if the cistern will just hold," Father said. "There may be some weak spots, and the water will seep away. Before I go to bed tonight, I'll measure the water level. Then I'll check it again in the morning."

Even before breakfast the next day, we gathered around while Father measured by putting the pole down through the small trap door in the platform. Hurrah! There was hardly a fraction of an inch difference from the other mark. Father primed the pump to fill the teakettle, and we girls took turns at the handle, being careful to catch every drop of the precious water.

"You must not drink from the pump," Father said. "It may be quite safe, but we'll take no chances in this hot weather. We'll boil it first, just as we have been doing."

That afternoon there was a flopping polliwog in my pail at the pump. I knew about polliwogs and was not frightened, but I needed no further reminders about not drinking from the pump.

Careful as we were, it wasn't long before the water was low in the cistern. Father hated to borrow a team and wagon again, so we decided to buy a horse he could drive with Duke to do the farm work. The old mare, Molly, did all she could do to raise her colt, and Father dared not work her. He heard of a piebald gelding for sale in the Coffee Flats and rode Duke over to buy him.

We soon knew why Doc had been sold. He was a dullard. He wasn't lazy. He was stupid. When orders got through to him, he was obedient and willing, but there was no way to hurry his comprehension. Duke was always alert, even when he was standing still, but Doc dozed off the minute he heard "Whoa" and dreamed till the reins were slapped on his back again. Duke walked quickly and eagerly, watching everything and listening to all sounds. Doc plodded beside him, oblivious to his surroundings. Duke was always a bit ahead, pulling more than his share of the load.

One day Father was cultivating corn when Duke suddenly shied and reared in the harness. Father shouted, "Whoa," wrapped the reins around the brake handle and hurried to the horses' heads. Duke trembled, but Doc just stood there, his foot on the tail of a rattlesnake. Before Father could do anything, the snake struck. Father grabbed Doc's bit and backed the team up, then ran as fast as he could the short distance to the house.

"This would be the day I'd forget to put my jackknife in my pocket," Father shouted as he dashed through the kitchen. "Doc's been bitten by a rattler! I must save him, if I can."

I ran with him back to the field, watching carefully for the snake, which must have slithered away.

Father had heard how it must be done. He made a deep cut just above the hoof where the fangs had pierced. Then he made another cut so there was an "X." When the blood began to flow, he unhitched the team and took them to the barn. Doc's hoof was bright red with blood, and Father was almost sobbing as he took off the harness and led the docile horse into the coolness of the barn.

"Put Duke out to pasture," he said to me. "I won't be needing him for awhile."

By morning Doc's leg was swollen to his shoulder, his head hung down, and his eyes were glazed by the fever and pain. Father used wet compresses on the wound and tried to get Doc to drink from a bucket. He worried and prayed. Doc was clumsy and dull witted, but we loved him and couldn't afford to lose him.

Doc suffered for three days before the swelling began to go down. Father waited many days before hitching him with Duke to finish the corn cultivating.

Another day in the fall, Father and I were on our way to the big water hole to get water for the cistern. Someone else was using Howell's tank wagon, so we had two wooden barrels in the spring wagon. We hoped to haul enough water to tide us over until the tank wagon was available. I held a galvanized pail on my lap with a rope attached to haul up the water.

As we rode along, we talked about how well Doc had recovered and how strong he was.

"If Doc hadn't been such an obedient, slow-witted creature, he never would have stopped so close to the rattlesnake," said Father. "As it is, it's a miracle we still have him. I sometimes wonder if he's deaf. I don't think Duke will ever get close enough to a rattler to be in any danger. Doc, you laggard, giddy up!" Father slapped the reins on Doc's fat back.

Water holes on the prairie are nothing more than washed-out low places in the sod where spring floods and summer cloudbursts have deposited water. Seldom more than a few feet deep, they may be quite wide and hold a quantity of water. This deep water hole was never known to go dry, and it had sweet water—not the brackish water often found in the holes. Since it was located on one of the lowest places on our land, Father wondered if it might not be spring fed. It was well known in the valley, and we weren't the only ones who drew drinking water from it. Cattle were carefully fenced out to protect it from contamination.

Father opened the gate, and we backed down the grassy bank that sloped gently to the water. Soon the wagon wheels were in the water and mud began splashing into the clear depths.

"Guess that's far enough. Whoa!" Father called. Doc didn't get the message and kept on backing, pulling Duke with him.

"Whoa! Whoa!" Father shouted, slapping the horses' backs with the reins.

The wagon went over the edge of a drop-off. With a jolt, the back wheels were almost submerged. Even though I clung to them with all my strength, the barrels slid along the bottom of the wagon box. I began slipping into the water with them!

"Papa! Papa!" I screamed.

Father was standing up and shouting at the horses, slapping the reins, trying to get them to stop backing. At my cry, he turned and snatched my sliding body. The barrels splashed into the water and, at the sound, the horses stopped, and then lunged forward up the bank. Father sprawled over the seat of the spring wagon, the reins over his shoulder still clutched in one hand. I lay stretched out in the bed of the wagon.

"You fool horses. Stand still! Whoa!" he cried and pulled me forward. "Lenna, are you hurt? You might have drowned!"

"I'm all right; just wet," I said.

The back of the wagon had been nearly submerged in the deep water. I had been so busy trying to keep the barrels from sliding out, I had had no time to be frightened, but now I shivered in Father's arms.

"We're going to try this again as soon as I capture those barrels," Father said. "That Doc is going to learn I'm boss. Now you climb out and go up there on the high bank until I get these barrels filled."

The barrels had floated across the water hole and were bobbing gently near the edge. Father walked around, pulled out the barrels, rolled them back to the wagon, and lifted them in. He backed the team up so the wheels were once again in the water, but this time the team stopped when Father shouted at them. They stood quietly just out of the water on the dry grass, as they were supposed to do. I watched Father toss the pail out into the clear, undisturbed water and draw it back with the rope.

As I dried out in the hot afternoon breeze, I wondered what Mother would think about the slightly muddy drinking water. However, I needn't have worried. By the time Father and

I emptied six barrels into the cistern, the water was so roiled up Mother wouldn't know whether we'd brought muddy water or just stirred up the silt in the cistern. That wasn't the only secret Father and I kept. He didn't want to worry Mother with the knowledge that I might have drowned. He promised to teach Verna and me how to swim.

Chapter 19

Ladies Aid Society

Mother was cleaning and baking, preparing for a gathering of the Valley Ladies Aid Society. This was the first time Mother had entertained since moving to the homestead, and she was happy and eager to have things as nice as she could. Father brought extra chairs from the haymow of the barn where our extra furniture was stored. Verna and I made the beds and dusted.

"We'll have to make fresh butter," Mother said.

Mother had devised a special cooling system for milk and butter. A Karo Syrup pail with a tight-fitting lid was lowered by rope into the depths of the cistern so that the pail was partly submerged in the cool water. But we had to churn often in hot weather, for butter quickly became rancid even when suspended in the water.

"Bring the sour cream from the cistern, please," she said to me.

We had no churn, but Mother had solved that problem too. The cream was sealed in a large, two-quart glass canning jar and laid in the seat of a rocking chair. Large muslin dish towels were tied around the jar and then to each arm and the back of the chair.

I sat on a stool beside the rocker and listened to the cream slap back and forth as I briskly rocked the chair. Though it was a hot morning, a cooling breeze sighed through the screen door. Fly paper hanging in a curl near the door swung back and forth almost in rhythm with the churning.

I picked up Roy, who had crawled toward the door, put him back on the blanket to play with his string of spools and continued with the churning. It wasn't long before the thud of the cream against the jar changed to the splash of the thinner buttermilk, and when I unwrapped the jar, there were the lumps of yellow butter.

"It's done, Mamma," I called.

"I'll work it in a minute," she said. "Pour off the buttermilk into a clean jar and put it into the cistern for Papa. While you're outside, please get me a quart jar of rabbit from the cave."

Mother stored many jars of canned jackrabbit steaks in the mounded, sod-roofed hole in the ground that Minnie had relied on in time of storm. Father hunted in cool weather whenever he had time, and the canned meat helped us stretch the grocery money. Mother planned to grind and season the rabbit and make sandwiches for the ladies.

"Whew," said Father as he banged the screen door behind him at noon. "Going to be hot today. Here's the mail."

"Well, sit right down and eat. All those women will be here before we know it," said Mother.

After the blessing, Father said, "I told Dad Jahns we were thinking of digging a well, and he said he's witched for water lots of times and has always been successful. I could hardly keep from smiling, but he was so sincere, I didn't."

To Father's surprise, Mother said, "If it gives him pleasure, why not let him try? Lots of people believe in it, even if we don't."

We hurried through dinner so Father could pick up Mrs. Stalford for the meeting. She didn't belong to the Ladies Aid Society, but she had once lived in the valley and knew everyone there. Plus, she was Mother's best friend. We girls were especially happy she was coming, because she would bring her daughter, Elsie. Taking care of Roy when he woke from his nap wouldn't be such a chore with Elsie there.

By two o'clock, our yard was full of buggies and horses, and the house was full of women. Elsie, Verna, and I played outside in the shade of the house. It was one of those days when according to Mother, "the shade of a two-by-four is appreciated." The morning breeze had disappeared, and the sun burned down from a cloudless sky.

In the late afternoon, Mother brought Roy out for us to care for. I followed her back into the house to get his toys from the lean-to bedroom. The ladies had put their hats there, and I noticed especially the one on the sewing machine. Big, red, silk flowers went all around the shiny straw crown. I picked it up and was turning it in my hands when, to my shock, I saw bedbugs scrambling for cover under the brim.

Our battle with bedbugs was a continuing fight. Mother thought she had the battle won when she cleaned and papered our first rooms so thoroughly. But every so often, a bug would be discovered and the hunt would begin again. Our beds stood in cans containing kerosene, just like the Clifton woman's. Mother regularly used corrosive sublimate on the mop boards and moldings and anywhere she thought the bugs might hide. She used gasoline in the creases and folded edges of the mattresses and was thankful that she and Father slept on a featherbed that gave the bugs few seams in which to hide. Hunting the bugs down had become almost an obsession with Mother.

Now, here before my eyes was evidence of a new invasion. I couldn't bother Mother with it now, but something had to be done—and fast. Could I get that hat outdoors without being seen? Any lady looking toward the lean-to kitchen would surely see me as I came out the bedroom door.

I snatched a pillowcase from the cupboard in the corner, stuffed the hat and invaders inside, and walked out of the house as nonchalantly as I could. I knew I mustn't put this hatchery anywhere near the baby playing on the blanket, yet I wanted to share this horrible secret with Verna and Elsie. I motioned to them to follow me around the corner of the house where no visitor could see. Father could have if he'd looked up, but he was busy building a shed down by the barn. The three of us looked down into the pillowcase and sure enough, my eyes hadn't deceived me. The bedbugs were still crawling around on the hat.

"Whose hat is it?" Elsie said.

"I don't know. It was just there on the sewing machine."

"What are you going to do with it?" Verna asked.

"I don't know," I said in a hoarse whisper.

"We'll just have to leave it out here," Elsie said. "Let's close it up tight and leave it right here on the ground in the sunshine. Maybe the bugs will roast to death."

She tied a knot in the open end of the pillowcase, placed the white bundle far out in the yard, and we went back to our play. Now and then we pondered on what we'd do about the hat when it came time for the women to go home, but there seemed no solution to the problem.

In the midst of an imaginary church service as Verna was intoning the number of the hymn to a well-dressed family of paper dolls, the screen door opened and Mrs. Cass and Mrs. Disbrow came out. Several other ladies followed close behind and headed for their waiting buggies. The hat lay in its white shroud in full view.

"But it must be here, Mrs. Batcher," Mother said. "I remember putting it on the sewing machine. Do you suppose someone picked it up by mistake? Let me look out in the other room."

There was more talk, and then Mother pushed open the screen door. "Lenna, did you see Mrs. Batcher's hat? I put it on the sewing machine, but it's gone. You didn't put it somewhere else, did you?"

I searched my mind for some way out but could only think to say, "Yes. I brought it out here. It's in that pillowcase over there."

Mother stared at the hat with an expression of disbelief. But then she turned to me with the slightest hint of a smile. "Here it is, Mrs. Batcher, out here. I guess the girls were admiring it. What a thing to do. Children do surprise us sometimes. I'm sure they haven't harmed it. They've kept it covered in a pillowcase. Bring it here, girls."

Mrs. Batcher was a large, older woman with a bulbous nose. She lumbered toward me, and I turned bright red with anxiety, but as she drew closer, I could see that her eyes were kind and forgiving. She took the hat from the pillowcase and put it on her stringy gray hair. Verna, Elsie, and I silently watched as she climbed laboriously into Mrs. Scott's buggy, and she and her colony of bedbugs rode away.

I turned expecting a scolding from Mother, but she had disappeared. Shrieks of laughter tumbled out from the house, and we girls picked up Roy and hurried inside. Mother and Mrs. Stalford were rocking back and forth in their chairs laughing.

When Mother could talk she explained, "Mr. and Mrs. Batcher are very old. You girls know how hard it is for me to fight those horrible bedbugs. Well, Mrs. Batcher is just too old to put up a good fight."

Mrs. Stalford picked up the story as Mother dissolved into laughter again. "Everyone knows their place is just crawling with bugs, and we all dread to have Mr. and Mrs. Batcher come visiting for fear they'll bring bedbugs along."

Mother wiped a tear from her eye with a lace handkerchief. "When Mrs. Batcher came today, I put her hat as far from the bed as possible—on the sewing machine. You solved the rest of the problem by taking the hat outdoors. You did just the right thing. Here I worried all afternoon about that hat, and all the time you had the problem solved for me. Why the pillowcase?"

I explained, and she said it was thanks to me that Mrs. Batcher had taken her well-traveled bugs back home. I already knew the battle was about to begin anew. If Mrs. Batcher left even one behind, Mother would hunt it down and train all her artillery on it by morning.

Chapter 20

Harvest

Bringing in the harvest

We had a bountiful crop of wheat in 1916, and prices were high. Father had complained a lot about the hot, dry summer, but once the wheat was cut, he took to worrying that it might rain. "I must get that grain shocked," Father said. "If it rains while it's still down, we'll lose it."

"I wouldn't worry," Mother said. "There's not a cloud in the sky, and it's hot already."

"Who knows how long our field will have to wait. I can't do it until I'm through traveling with the harvesters," said Father. The farmers in the area pitched in to cut everyone's wheat, but it was up to each man to do the shocking—gathering the bundles and piling them—or hire someone to get it done. Most of our crop, except for one small field, was already in the barn, and we couldn't afford any help to finish the job.

"You know, if you'd show us how, I think the girls and I could do that small field," Mother said.

Father's face darkened. Wide-eyed, he thundered, "I'll not have my wife working in the fields like a peasant woman."

Mother examined her hands in her lap. The shadow of a smile crossed her lips, but she said nothing.

"It's bad enough, having to live in this poor house," Father said. "But work in the fields? Never!"

Mother tried to break in, but he kept right on in his loud, preaching voice. "Think what the neighbors would say. I can just hear them. Besides, the work is too hard."

"Who cares what the neighbors think," Mother said with the quiet, reasonable tone she took to win most disagreements. "We can work until we get tired, and then do more the next day. How else can we get the fields shocked otherwise?"

"I just won't have it," Father said, but I could tell she was wearing him down.

"Now stop worrying. We'll figure it out some way," Mother said.

Mother prevailed. The next morning, as Father was heading out with the other men, she said, "Now, don't worry about us.

We'll be all right. By the way, what wages are you planning to pay your three fine farm hands?" She laughed and kissed him. The evening before, Father had taken us down to the field, grumbling the whole way. Verna, Mother, and I learned the best way to pick up the bundles of wheat, lean two together, and stack other bundles around them to make a shock. It seemed simple enough.

"Don't forget to watch for rattlesnakes," Father said. "Just across the fence from that field is where Dad Jahns and I dug up that nest of them."

He kissed us children, climbed into Mr. Sykes' wagon, and waved goodbye. Mother went inside and finished her chores, but we girls stayed at the door and waved at Father as long as he would wave back.

"Girls, you'd better get the dishes washed. We should get down to the field as soon as we can, for it's going to be a scorcher today. I'll get Roy ready, and then we'll make some sandwiches and lemonade and be off."

"Wish I had some overalls," she said as she made sandwiches. Papa wouldn't hear of such a thing, of course. Guess my black-and-white checked dress will do. You girls must wear long-sleeved blouses with your overalls and put on those black-stocking wristlets I made for you."

"But we'll be so hot," Verna said, whining.

"Hot or not, we've got to do all we can to keep the wheat beards out. They are miserable when you get them inside next to your skin."

"Wheat beards?" Verna said, pulling a long face to make a joke of it.

"Those stickers we got in our stockings last night, down in the field," I said, a bit scornful of Verna's ignorance.

We were used to wearing the wristlets to keep our arms from getting too tanned. Mother was determined we'd look like fair-skinned city girls, even though we lived on the prairie. Holes cut in the heels of old black lisle stockings served as thumb holes, and the toe was snipped off to free our fingers. Elastic bands held the stocking legs above our elbows, and cotton work gloves covered our hands. Wide-brimmed straw hats kept our heads cool and our faces protected.

"It's a good thing Papa can't see us now," Mother said, sporting the same makeshift sun protection. "He wouldn't think his womenfolk were very beautiful today, would he?"

We scrambled into the back of the spring wagon with Roy, and Mother took the reins. Duke and Doc pulled us down through the pasture where the spicy, sweet fragrance of hay lingered from the last cutting. Mother had rigged a wooden crate for Roy to play in as we worked, and it slid back with a screech as the team pulled us up the steep incline. The long leaves in the corn patch whispered and rustled mysteriously in the hot breeze. Beyond that, dry, golden mounds of wheat spread out before us.

The morning was already half gone when Mother unhitched Duke and Doc and tied them to a wagon wheel. I hated to think of them standing in the heat all day with the harness on. Mother must have been thinking about it too, for she looked at me and said, "We probably won't work too long today. We'll test ourselves. Find out how much we can do without getting too tired."

She climbed back into the wagon and made Roy comfortable in the big crate. He protested the confinement, for he had enjoyed the ride on my lap, babbling the whole way. As soon as he found his string of wooden spools, he was content. Mother fastened the mosquito netting securely over the top of the box, and we headed into the field.

The soft ground still bore the marks of the cleats on the binder's iron wheels as it rolled across the field cutting and tying the heavy-headed grain into bundles. The remaining stubble marched toward us in dizzying rows fanning out in every direction. The twine cut into our hands as we dragged the heavy sheaves along over the rough ground. It didn't take us long to become fairly efficient at setting up the shocks.

At noon we stopped and ate Mother's creamy cheese sandwiches half melted by the sun. We gulped the cool, tangy lemonade and savored the sugary aftertaste. Mother lifted Roy out of his box and wiped his pink, sweaty face. She twisted a moist lock of his hair into a curl on the top of his head and said, "Hi, kewpie!" He had been scolding and complaining, but he cheered up once he drank the milk we'd kept cooled in the kettle. He soon drifted to sleep on the quilt in the bottom of the crate, and we returned to work.

The picnic atmosphere we'd started out with that morning began to wear off as our muscles began to ache. Perspiration soaked our blouses, and the wheat beards crept into the tops of our shoes and pinched us through our socks. The wind kicked up and sent dust and pollen blowing, which made me sneeze. We no longer chattered as we worked. It took all our strength just to keep going.

"Girls! Don't move! I hear a rattler!"

Mother was a few feet ahead of me. She stood stock still, her back to me. Verna stopped to our right. I was dragging a bundle, struggling to hold it by the twine cutting into my hand, but I stopped in midstep. So did Verna.

"I can't see it, but I can hear it!"

The wind rattled the corn nearby. The afternoon sun burned through my hat, and rivulets of sweat coursed down my neck. Yellow and brown grasshoppers buzzed and flipped past me. Roy talked to himself in his box. Doc jingled his harness and stomped a foot against the biting flies. I heard all these sounds—not the rattle of the snake.

"Maybe it was just a grasshopper," Verna said in a tight, thin voice.

"Don't move," Mother said.

Our eyes searched the ground all around us for sight of the snake. I didn't dare wipe the sweat running into my eyes. A wheat beard pierced the tender skin at the bend of my elbow. I did not move.

"It's very near," Mother said.

I heard the faint rattling like far-off music.

The bundle grew heavier in my hand. Needles of pain stitched up my arm. Sweat dripped off my nose.

"Remember to move away from the snake when we see it. It will want to get away. It doesn't want to hurt us," Mother said. Her long black and white skirt flapped about her legs like a flag in a stiff breeze.

I heard the rattle again. Then I saw the snake right behind Mother. It coiled its gray-diamond back and lifted its flat head toward Mother's blowing skirt.

"I hear it again!" cried Mother.

My mind raced, and yet, I couldn't think. If I shouted, Mother would jump, but would she jump in the right direction? I froze.

"Watch out! It must be very close," Mother cried.

My throat tightened. I tried to speak, but nothing came out.

The snake's head parried with the billowing skirt, diving toward Mother, then back, then so near I knew it must strike at any second.

"Mother," I said in a hoarse whisper. "It's behind you." The words stuck to my tongue. I had to push them out. "At the hem of your skirt." The snake's head darted again. Too close. "Jump!" I screamed.

The snake reared back and hurled itself at Mother. She leapt, and the fangs caught her skirt. Venom leeched into the black and white plaid. The snake clung to her, its sinuous body hanging limp in the fold of her skirt.

I was still frozen in place when it dropped off and writhed itself into an S that wove away through the stubble.

I let go of the grain bundle and ran to her. "Did it bite you?"

"No. I don't think so," she said. Her voice shook and her white face glowed with sweat.

A powerful shiver overtook me, and I began to sob in relief as much as fright.

"Stop your crying," she said. "I'm all right. Watch where the snake goes. We must kill it." She tossed about looking for a weapon, but I could only stare at her, paralyzed once again.

"Find a stone, a stick, something," she shouted. But the snake was gone. We had to give up and let it glide away into the prairie grass.

As we rode away, I looked back at the sturdy grain shocks we had built that day. I moved closer to my mother and bent my face to touch Roy's head with my cheek as he sat in my lap. His touch always gave me a sense of peace, but this time, underneath it, a rage seethed at the snake that had struck out at my mother.

Chapter 21

The Wheat Check

Verna and I were finishing the breakfast dishes when the threshing rig came over the last rise along the section line. The machine pulled itself ponderously up out of the low places in the prairie between us and Dad Jahns' corner. Black smoke poured from the engine, and the huge wheels turned slowly along the trail beside the barbed-wire fence. By the time it reached our yard, it had grown to monstrous proportions.

The steam engine whistled three times, and the rig made a wide circle through the gate and stopped near the barn. Red fire glowed in the thresher's heart. It coughed and throbbed and threw cinders from its smokestack, and the long, shiny blower, folded back along the separator, waggled with every vibration.

Mr. Sykes and his four sons arrived in two lumber wagons, and Mr. Cass and his two boys drove in with a bundle wagon. Dad Jahns rode in with Mr. Howell and Myron driving their white mules. We girls watched the men put the long belt in place on the thresher, mesmerized by the scene.

"There'll be time later on to watch," Mother said. Come help me now." Then she remembered to remind us two about our manners. "Did you say hello to Eric and Arnold and the Sykes boys?"

"We waved. They're working," Verna said.

All morning we stole looks at the threshing, even though Father had told us it was no place for girls. The straw stack grew till it rose higher than the barn. Yellow grain flowed out of the separator into the wagons. Father drove load after load to the scales at Disbrow's store, then to the freight cars on the siding, where it joined the grain already delivered from the other farms.

At about ten o'clock, Father came to the house and said, "They're going to be through early. You'll have to hurry dinner."

"I'll do my best," Mother said. The roasted chickens were browned and fragrant with rosemary and butter when we heard a change in the sounds coming from the yard.

"The threshing machine is leaving," Verna exclaimed.

"I tried to get them to stay for dinner," Father said, "but they thought it was too early to quit. They're going over to Cavinder's next."

"But what will I do with all this food?" Mother wailed.

"James Sykes and his boys are still here. He said it would be a hot day in the winter before he'd help Cavinder with threshing or anything else."

Soon we heard the men laughing and talking as they washed up. Tall James Sykes stooped to go through the door. Father and the four boys followed close behind. They all joked and laughed as they sat down to eat.

In no time, there wasn't a biscuit, potato, bit of meat, or piece of pie left. Mother looked at the empty table and said, "I never dreamed men could eat that much, let alone boys! As it was, there wasn't enough gravy to go around. Whew! The Lord was surely with me when that crew of men went on to Cavinder's."

Days later, Mother stood by the table opening the mail. She tore the end off a long white envelope, pulled out a slip of paper, and stared at it. "Go get Papa. Quick."

Mother looked so strange. I didn't stop to ask questions. I ran to the barn as fast as I could. As Father ran back with me, he cried "Is she sick? Is something wrong?"

"I don't think so. She looked kind of happy, I think."

Mother threw her arms around Father when he came through the door. She waved the slip of paper before his face.

"Look, Joe. Just look!"

He snatched the paper out of her hand.

"It's the wheat check." She almost squealed with excitement. "Read it!"

Father read out loud. "One thousand and sixty dollars."

"Imagine. One thousand and sixty dollars!" She twirled in a little dance. "I never thought I'd ever see so much money all at once. Thank the Lord!"

That night at the supper table, instead of the usual blessing, we all sang, "Praise God from whom all blessings flow."

Chapter 22

Father Buys Some Cattle

I bought two cows and a bull calf," Father said, back from a closing-out sale near Rumford. "There's no way to get them home except to drive them. I'll need help. Lenna, how would you like to ride with me to get them tomorrow?"

"But there's only one saddle, and it's seven miles," protested Mother.

"We'll put the saddle on Duke and the blanket and surcingle on Doc. He has a fat back. We'll take turns."

"I'd like to go!" I decided at once.

Father built a cow shed back of the barn in the shelter of the straw stack. He whistled while he worked, and as I helped him clinch nails in the boards, I learned to whistle a soft tune through my teeth. He'd been watching for sales of cattle and prepared for ten cows, for it seemed this would be a minimum if we were going to ship cream.

We set out in the chill dawn. Doc's "jog-trot," as Father called it, was anything but smooth, and Duke's western saddle tired Father. Western-style riding seemed ungraceful and undignified to him. He tried it but soon switched to the English style he had learned as a boy. This was hard on his knees and upper legs for the width of the western saddle at either side of the pommel didn't allow for going up and down with the rhythm of the horse's stride.

We walked our horses into the yard in Rumsford, past men loading their wagons with the machinery and livestock they'd purchased the day before. After quite some time, Mr. Shreve saw Father.

"Reverend O'Neill, you and your daughter better plan to spend the night. There are several loads to be handled yet, and by the time we get around to cutting out your stock, it will be almost dark. Things are pretty much of a jumble up at the house, but we'll find a bed somewhere."

I was so tired I hardly knew what I ate at the crowded supper table, and the cigar smoke that filled the air in the small house nauseated me.

"You sleep here," Mrs. Shreve said, waving us into the front bedroom. In a daze of exhaustion, I barely registered that most of the others at the house would sleep on the floor. She had shown her respect by giving the preacher the best bedroom.

After reading his pocket Testament and saying a goodnight prayer for us both, Father wrapped himself in a quilt and sat in the rocking chair instead of lying down beside me.

"But, Papa, you'll be so tired," I whispered to him in the quiet of the bedded-down house.

"Probably won't sleep anyway," he said. "Get your rest, my girl."

The ride home was worse than the day before. "Wish we could go faster," I said. "I can hardly wait to show Mother and Verna our cattle. Wonder how Jersey Belle will act around another cow. She's so ornery!"

"In Ireland we had a cow almost like this brindle cow. She was the pet of all of us boys. We thought she gave the best milk of any of my father's herd. She had a crooked horn, I remember. Let's call this cow Brindle, shall we?"

"Tell me more about Ireland, Papa," I said. "Did you have horses to ride like Duke and Doc?"

"No, but we had a pony we could ride. His name was Dan. Most of the time we drove him hitched to our cart. Over there, it was called a 'car.' The seats were back to back, and we rode sideways above high wheels. Only the driver faced forward. There were usually two or three dogs following the car. With nine children in the family, we had to have enough pets to go around."

The forenoon slipped by with his storytelling. The cattle wearied and tried to stop to graze, but we urged them on.

"What shall we call the red cow?" Father said. "Let's think of something red. How about Ruby, Rosie, or Cherry?"

"Cherry, I think. The calf should have a name too. Doesn't he moo funny—way up high like that," I said. "He's probably lonesome for the calves he's been with. Since he has such a peculiar voice, let's call him after some singer. John McCormick is my favorite, but that wouldn't be a good name for a calf. I know! Let's call him Caruso!"

We both laughed. Caruso he was, and that hoarse, high-pitched bellow echoed through several generations of the O'Neills's herd.

Chapter 23

The Runaway

The wheat money transformed our humble homestead into a real working farm. Father was a natural carpenter, and he had no trouble building a tall horse barn with stalls for four horses and a cow barn where our three newly acquired milk cows lived. Thanks to a new law that allowed it, we doubled our acreage with grazing land. More than ever, Father needed a reliable team of horses.

Late one afternoon in early autumn, Father rode into the yard with two horses tied to the back of the wagon. "Got the best bargain at the sale," he said. Mother looked skeptical, but Verna and I raced out to meet the new team.

The tall bay was called Jim, and the shorter, white one was Jay. The seven-mile trot left Jim winded—wheezing and blowing, but Jay looked spirited and strong. He got skittish when we approached, and when we led him down to the pasture, he reared at the barbed-wire fence and shied away from it as if it would attack.

In the days that followed, we discovered that Jay was almost impossible to catch in the pasture. It took urging to the point of exasperation to get him to step over the drop gate, and once he was across, he bolted in fear. When Father did catch him and put the harness on him, Jay pranced and fought the bit, which irritated Father to no end.

"If I didn't need them so much, I'd get rid of those two in a hurry. How could I have made such a mistake!" Nevertheless, Father put Jim and Jay to work hauling the wagon. One cold morning in October, he set out for Edgemont to pick up lumber, coal, and groceries.

Mother complained of a backache and spent most of the day doing hand sewing and mending. Verna and I did our lessons under Mother's watchful eye. It was cozy and warm inside. Except for an occasional trip to the barn to gather wood scraps for the fire, we hardly ventured out. Gray clouds settled lower over the prairie as the day wore on. After noon, the wind picked up, and in a while, a few snowflakes skittered against the windowpanes.

"It's getting dark early today," Mother said. "I wish Papa were home. He'll be cold and tired after riding in that open lumber wagon. Let's help him by getting the cows in and ready for milking." I glanced at Verna, who was curled up under a blanket looking like she didn't want to go out there any more than I did.

"Wish I'd insisted that he take the Irish blanket to help keep him warm," Mother said. "I'm so afraid he'll take cold and be sick again."

Father's health was still the chief worry of our family. He'd had a good summer with less sleeplessness than usual, but he still coughed a lot. Mother tried to fatten him up but succeeded only in increasing her own girth.

"If only you didn't work so hard," Mother often said to him.

"The work is there to be done," he'd say. "I really am better than I was last year. Give me time."

By four o'clock, Father still wasn't home. We kept a look-out for him, watching the horizon at Roberts Hill. Verna and I had gone out together to get the cows in the barn, and my fingers burned from the cold.

At last I saw him, or I thought I did.

Jim and Jay were running toward home at full gallop. The lumber wagon swayed back and forth behind them, strewing lumber and groceries. There was no sight of Father.

Prince and Queen barked frantically in the yard. "Papa's not in the wagon!" I yelled. Mother dropped her sewing.

We ran out just as the team turned into the yard. They tried to stop, but the momentum of the wagon forced them almost to the opposite fence. Jim's throat was rattling and both horses had raised a foaming sweat. The wagon's end gate was gone. An empty 100-pound sack of sugar lay flattened in the wagon box, and a roll of barbed wire was caught up on a nail. Nothing else survived the trip.

Mother picked up the reins and tied them around the wheel brake. She backed the team to the hitching post, and I snapped the tie rope to Jim's bit.

"Lenna, I'll need you to help me hitch the team to the spring wagon. I must go back to look for Papa." She ran to the house and reappeared in her warm coat and mittens.

"Verna, get me the Irish blanket, the quilts off our beds, bring the pillows too. Get dish towels I can tear up if Papa needs bandages."

Verna stood stock still and open mouthed.

"Now don't be frightened. It's just best that I go prepared. Lenna, fill both hot-water bottles from the teakettle." She was harnessing the horses without me, talking a blue streak.

I knew from watching Father how to hitch and unhitch a team, but Mother flew at the unhitching and ignored me. I held the horses' heads as she snapped the tugs to the whiffletrees of the spring wagon. "Get more wood for the fire and put the kettle to boil."

Mother spread the blanket Verna brought out in the bottom of the spring wagon. She placed the hot-water bottles between the pillows and put the quilts on top. Then she climbed onto the seat and called out, "Take good care of Roy and pray that Papa's safe," as she drove away.

I wanted to cry but knew I mustn't. "I'll build up the fire," I said to Verna, who looked as white as the snow gathering on the ground. "You go pump a pail of water. I'll get coal for the fire. Hurry up so you can stay with Roy while I go outside." Even in her coat and mittens, Verna shivered, but she obeyed.

Once we'd done everything Mother had asked, we took turns peering out the parlor window, which had a view to the lane. Wind rattled the house. In the glowing dusk, with nothing to do but wait, time slowed. Little fears crept into my heart. What if it got dark before Mother found Father? Would Jim and Jay run away again when they came upon whatever had frightened them? What if Father was terribly hurt? Could Mother get him into the spring wagon? I kept my fears to myself, knowing that Verna, no doubt, had her own. The simmering of the kettles of water on the glowing stove seemed the only cheerful things left in the world.

Prince whined to go out. Verna slammed the door behind him to shut out the cold.

"Let's set the table for supper," I said. "I'll make some tea."

I put the tea in the tea ball, hooked it over the edge of the teapot, and was pouring the boiling water when Prince barked. We ran to the window and cupped our hands against the glass. There they were!

Father was driving, and Mother was huddled beside him holding a basket of groceries on her lap. Lumber stuck out over the end gate and crosswise above the wheels. The horses' heads drooped as they plodded into the yard.

"Oh, my good girls!" Mother said, squeezing through the doorway with her arms loaded. "We came back as soon as we could, but there was all that lumber to pick up and groceries to gather."

She picked up Roy and gave him a hug and a kiss.

"Papa's all right?" I asked.

"Yes, thank the Lord! He isn't hurt at all. But he's surely cross at those horses."

She took off her coat and hung it on the hook. "We won't need the hot water now. What a blessing he wasn't hurt." She pulled on her apron and brushed back her flyaway hair. "I'll start supper. Maybe Papa will want to eat before he milks. He's so tired." She fluttered around the kitchen in high spirits. "Good, you've made tea. He can have some of that at least."

"Where did you find Papa?" I said. "We want to know what happened."

"About halfway between Bushnell's and Barber's, I saw Papa walking toward me along the side of the road. It looked like he was waving a white flag and that gave me a start, but then I saw it was the torn sack of flour. I was so relieved I almost cried. Then I laughed. He looked like a ghost with flour spilled down his coat and blown into his hair and eyebrows and mustache."

Verna and I giggled. All the fear drained out of me with the laughter.

Mother scrubbed potatoes and didn't even ask me to help. "You know how stern Papa gets when he's angry. When I reached him and he saw I was laughing, he said, 'Woman, what's so funny?' That made me laugh more, and then I was crying too. When he climbed into the spring wagon, you may be sure I hugged him good."

I finished setting the table as she talked, and I savored the warmth of the kitchen and my mother's musical tone as she related her tale.

"When Papa saw the blankets, pillows, and all, he realized how fearful we had been. That lightened his cross look, but he was still angry at the team, and he couldn't see the humor in the sight of him covered with the flour. I'm sure it wasn't funny. I was just silly, because I was so relieved."

When Father came in, he reached out his arms to her and embraced her even before he took off his flour-covered coat. He didn't let her go for a very long time, and when he finally did, he bent down and hugged each of us.

"That fool Jay," he said. "Why I ever bought him, I'll never know."

Mother handed Father a cup of tea.

"Oh, Dearie. What a loss of food and money."

"Maybe we haven't lost as much as you think. Most of the groceries are here. Just be thankful the Lord kept you safe."

"Thanks to you too. I had no idea you were so expert at hitching and unhitching a team."

Mother smiled. "You seem to forget that I was a Nebraska farm girl a long time before I met up with the green Irishman I married."

Chapter 24

Sister

Helen Jenkins

Mother looked up from Dr. Quivey's letter and turned shining eyes to Father. "Listen to this. 'We have an eleven-year-old girl who, it seems to me, belongs with you. The child's father deserted the mother some years back. The mother worked desperately to make a home for her daughter, but she died three weeks ago.'"

"Hmm." Father's eyes didn't leave his newspaper.

"Dr. Quivey reminds me that I promised I would take a child when I could."

"Well, you can't," Father said, still keeping his nose in the paper. "I guess three womenfolk are about enough for a man."

Mother persisted. "She sounds like a nice little girl. He must think this child needs us particularly. I wonder—it seems a shame—we do have room."

Father's negative reaction didn't stop Mother from suggesting they think about adopting this orphan girl, which meant she'd give him some time to come around. She recruited us as allies in her cause. "Do you think you might like a big sister?"

"Oh, yes!" we both cried.

It was several days before Father grudgingly agreed to send for her, but he continued to voice his misgivings. Four days after Mother sent the letter to the Children's Home Finding Society, the station agent at Provo telephoned.

"Mrs. O'Neill, I have a telegram for you. Omaha, Nebraska, November twelve, nineteen sixteen. Stop. Helen Jenkins arrives Provo November thirteen at four twenty. Stop. Bless you. Stop. Dr. E. P. Quivey."

"My goodness. We hadn't expected her so soon," Mother said, her voice ringing.

"Your new sister will be here tomorrow afternoon," she said passing through the parlor. "Mind Roy. I must go tell Papa. My what a lot we have to do before tomorrow."

Verna and I looked at each other. A new sister tomorrow!

"What's her name?" Verna asked me.

"Helen. Didn't you hear Mother say it?"

"But that's your name."

"Yes, but mine's Helen Anna. Everybody calls me Lenna anyway. I'll be Lenna, and she can be Helen."

"I don't think we should have two Helens." Verna could be stubborn that way.

Mother came sailing back in. "Maybe she'll want to change her name," she said.

We helped Mother rearrange the furniture to make room for our new sister. Everything was ready when Father drove into the yard with her. The house shone. Our dresses were washed and starched. Our hair was freshly braided. Even our dolls were dressed up for the occasion.

Mother put an arm around Helen and led her into the house, while Father drove the Model T into the garage.

"We're so glad you're here," Mother said. She pulled me in. "This is Lenna," then gestured toward Verna, who, true to her open, friendly nature, already stood by Helen's side, fidgeting with excitement. "And this is Verna."

Helen Jenkins studied us with hooded brown eyes. Her lips formed a straight line dead set against the weakest smile. She was slim and pale and stood taller than Verna and me. Her dark hair formed two fat braids down her back. A faded red gingham dress peeked out from under a dull gray coat, and black wool stockings, mended at the bony knees, covered her stick-thin legs.

"Did you have a nice trip?" Mother asked, betraying her nervous energy. "Isn't it exciting to ride on a train?" Helen remained silent in the face of Mother's questions, which hung in the air like so much wet laundry. Mother ignored her poor manners and bustled while putting away Helen's coat and bonnet.

The girl sat on the edge of the chair and stared about the room.

Verna held out her doll. "This is Flora. I got her for my birthday. See, her name is here on her neck." She laid the doll in Helen's lap. "You can play with her. I have a rag doll too. Did you bring your doll?"

Helen shook her head.

"You can have one of ours. Come see which one you'd like," Verna said, bouncing from one leg to the other.

Father came in carrying a small cardboard box tied with string. "Here are your things, Helen," he said, setting the box down on the table.

"It's going to be a cold night. As soon as I get these clothes changed, let's get at the chores. Lenna, you feed the chickens. Verna, you get the eggs."

"And Helen can help me get supper," Mother said quickly. "She and I want to get acquainted."

In a few days, Helen was talking as much as any of us. It was as though we had always had an older sister. Verna and I adored her. We called her Bessie instead of Helen, after her mother. Helen loved hearing her mother's name.

"My best girl in Ireland was Bessie Fitselle," Father said. "Now you're one of my best girls. That's just the right name for you."

Bessie settled right in to helping with the chores. She trimmed the wicks and washed and polished the lamp chimneys, relieving Mother of that duty. With Verna's or my help, she brought in the heavy scuttles of coal for the two stoves, and Father taught all three of us how to milk the cows.

Bessie never showed much enthusiasm about anything, but she was willing and gentle. She didn't talk about the past, except to answer Mother's questions. Her box held three things of her mother's that she treasured—a brass thimble with green-and-white enamel trim, a beautiful small two-handled vase with painted figures, and a tiny glass cup. Bessie kept these treasures carefully wrapped and stowed away in a small box, and we respected her right to possessions of her own.

At Christmastime, even though Father was no longer the minister in Edgemont, we received the usual missionary box from the East. Aunt Harriet had seen to it that we weren't forgotten. A soft wool cap and scarf was labeled with Bessie's name. She was happier about this than about any other gift.

In January, Bessie caught cold and developed an ear infection. It caused her a lot of pain and constant drainage. Dr. Thompson tried to treat it, but it wouldn't clear up. Bessie grew more pale and silent as the weeks went on, but she seldom complained. Mother kept her inside for fear she'd chill and have a relapse. Even with such precautions, the earaches worsened. I often awoke late at night to the sound of Mother telling Bessie stories in a soft, whispering voice as Bessie laid on a hot-water bottle for some slight relief. Mother's soothing voice helped to keep her mind off the dreadful ache.

We did our schoolwork each morning, but Bessie had little interest or energy for it. She was a poor reader and hopelessly lost in arithmetic. Mother worried and worked with her—and loved her. We all longed to make her happy and well. When Father said, "Bessie, my love," it was with special tenderness.

On the first Sunday in March, Father suggested we all go to Edgemont for Sunday school and church.

"My back aches too bad," Mother said. "But the girls can go. Bessie too, if she wraps up. The ride in the sunshine and fresh air will do you all good." Bessie had gradually improved, but Mother still hovered over her, afraid of a relapse. "Girls, you try to remind Bessie to keep her ears covered. We don't want a sick girl again."

"That scarf tied around my head looks awful," Bessie complained. "Verna and Lenna don't have to. Besides, my ears don't hurt anymore."

"Better be safe than sorry. You can take the scarf off before you go into the church," said Mother. "But you put it on again before the drive home."

On the ride home, treacherous March winds blew strong and cold. I don't think Bessie meant to disobey Mother. She just forgot to wrap up in that scarf, and by late afternoon, she was crying with the pain in her ears.

All that night Mother went back and forth with hot-water bottles for Bessie. She sat by her bed and rubbed her thin hands, talking to her softly. The next morning, Bessie was burning with fever. For three days, she alternately cried and dozed. Verna and I tiptoed about and tried to keep Roy amused and quiet.

Father kept finding reasons to come back to the house so he could look in on her. "I need to fix the fence at the bottom of the pasture, but I won't go that far from the house as long as she is so sick," he told Mother.

On the third day, Mother called the doctor. He promised to come out that afternoon. Father said he'd go ahead and fix that fence and asked if he could take me along. I longed to escape all the worry that hovered around Bessie and crept into every corner of the house.

Mother agreed, and I whooped with joy, but I protested when she insisted I wear layers of clothes to keep me warm. "I declare, Lenna, you'd think you would have learned something from what Bessie did to herself," Mother scolded. "Put on that cap as I said. And put the sweater under your coat too."

"I don't see why Mama gets so cross with me these days. Seems I can't do anything right," I grumbled to Father as we headed for the pasture.

A warm south wind had melted most of the snow, and we walked swiftly over the spongy prairie sod.

"It won't be long before things will start growing," Father said. "The ground isn't completely thawed, but soon there'll be stirrings in all the roots."

When we arrived at the sagging fence, Father slipped the heavy wire stretcher off his shoulder and laid it on the ground. I set the bag of staples and the hammer down beside it, and when I straightened up, Father gripped both of my arms and said, "My girl, I have something very important to tell you."

My heart lurched and my head reared back, as if that would enable me to escape whatever bad news he had.

He pulled the stapler out of his pocket. "We'll have to work while I talk, but I want you to listen carefully."

I gave him a slow, reluctant nod.

"First, let me show you what we have to do here. All the staples on these posts have to be pulled so we can tighten the barbed wire from here to the corner post. Then when I get the stretcher on the wire and have it pulled tight, you must lift the wire to the right height on the post, and I'll hammer the staples. Do you understand?"

I nodded.

Father set to work yanking out the staples, and I hovered at his side.

"Now, what I'm about to tell you must be a secret between us for awhile. You mustn't tell Bessie or Verna, not until Mama wants you to." He handed me a pile of rusty staples. "I'm telling you now, because I want you to know why your dear Mother is cross and irritable lately."

My cheeks grew hot, and my mind raced to Father's health and other sickness and Bessie and money worries I'd overheard.

"She loves you and your sisters and Roy very much, but she has so many backaches and troubles she can hardly stand it." He stopped his work and turned. "Have you guessed that we're going to have a new baby at our house one of these days?"

That had definitely not occurred to me. I couldn't remember Mother even hinting of such a thing, but the relief made me giddy.

Father placed the stretcher on the wire and pulled. I held the wire level, but my hand shook a little, and I had a hard time standing still. Father had confided in me. I felt so grown up. A new baby was coming. I trembled with excitement. "I knew Mamma was getting awfully fat, but I didn't think about a baby."

"Yes, indeed." He gave the pulley a hard yank.

"When will the baby come?"

"Maybe this week." He hammered in the staples. "Almost any time now."

I held up the next wire, and he stretched it taught. "So you see, we have to be careful that Mama doesn't overdo. You girls must help her even more than you do now, especially with Bessie so sick. You must think of all the things that Bessie has been doing for Mama, and you do them till Bessie gets well."

I thought of all the chores that Bessie was supposed to do like keeping the lamp chimneys cleaned. It was so easy to break the glass. I worried that I wouldn't do a good job but promised to do my best.

When the last staple was driven, Father surveyed the taut fence with satisfaction. "That will do for awhile. Just in time too. I think that's Dr. Thompson's auto coming down the lane."

We hurried back across the low pasture and up toward our house. A north wind cut through my jacket and the sweater underneath. Moisture from the brown winter grass shone on my overshoes. A film of water ready to spill over and wash down the valley when spring finally broke glistened on the thawing ice in the water holes. I stomped on the patches of snow sheltered beneath the sagebrush and skipped on ahead of Father. Even with Bessie so ill, the land and I were brimming with joyous expectation.

Dr. Thompson snapped his black bag shut. "Your girl must go to a hospital at once. I suspect spinal meningitis."

"But where can we take her?" Mother cried. "It's twenty-eight miles to Hot Springs."

He slipped on his black jacket. "The roads to Hot Springs are impassable. Between the thaw and the rain, no wagon can get up Gull's Hill. Could you go by train?" He shook his head. "No, that's no good. Today's train has already gone. We can't wait until tomorrow."

Father paced, his heels knocking against the wood floor. "Do you suppose we could flag the train at Provo and get her on the flyer to Omaha?" he said.

"What time does the flyer go through?" Dr. Thompson said.

"About four o'clock."

"We must do it."

"It's almost two o'clock now. How can I get us both ready for the trip on time?" Mother said, her voice shrill with fright.

"You aren't going to try, Mrs. O'Neill. You know you can't go on such a trip just now."

I blushed, knowing what "just now" meant.

"I must go," Father said. "But how can I leave you here alone? Tomorrow is Sunday."

"Isn't there someone you could ask to go with her? She's too ill to be sent off alone, but neither of you should go."

"If we wire Dr. Quivey," Mother said, talking low, almost to herself, "he can make arrangements at the hospital." She rose from the table and went to the phone. "I'll ask Mrs. Disbrow to go with Bessie tonight. She could come right back on tomorrow morning's train."

So, it was arranged. Father sent the telegram to Dr. Quivey. There was no time to wait for a response. Mother packed a small bag for Bessie. She dressed her, lifting her limp arms, letting her lay back again against the pillows while she buttoned her up and put on her stockings and shoes. Mother put on her own coat and hat. Father wrapped Bessie in the Irish blanket and carried her to the car. I held Roy up to see as Verna and I waved goodbye, tears rolling in great drops down our cheeks.

Mother and Father were back from Provo by five o'clock. At a quarter to seven, the telephone rang. Father answered. He turned to us, his face lit by the lamplight, tears welling up in his eyes.

"Mrs. Disbrow wired. Bessie died before they reached Alliance. They took her off the train there."

We held on to each other and wept, and I sank into darkness, the deepest sadness I'd ever known.

Chapter 25

Dorothy is Born

The wind shifted the next day. With Bessie's passing, spring receded, and the prairies froze again. Fine pellets of snow and sleet brushed the frosted windowpanes.

Father had taken the train to Alliance for Bessie's funeral. We could not stand to have her buried with none of us there. We were having our sandwiches and milk after helping Mother with the washing all morning. "We're all tired from the anxieties of the last few days," Mother said. "Let's all lie down while Roy takes his nap."

Exhausted as I was, I couldn't sleep. I went to the kitchen table and read a story instead. Mother rested only a few minutes before she joined me.

"Papa said he told you about the baby coming," she said. "I'm glad. With Papa gone, I'll rely on you should the baby start to come."

My stomach knotted, but my heart swelled. I was only nine years old, but Mother believed she could rely on me.

"Would you know how to call the doctor, if you had to?"

"I think so." My voice fluttered, much as I tried to sound self-assured.

"I'll write down the number here on the outside of this envelope. You put it on top of the phone so you'll know exactly where it is. Ring one long ring for the telephone central and tell her this number. She'll get Dr. Thompson for you."

I reached on tiptoes to place the envelope on the telephone.

"If you can't get the doctor, you must call Mrs. Stalford, and if that fails, you must ring the general alarm—ten short rings—remember?"

I nodded.

She went to the bookshelf and retrieved the big, green doctor book she used to look up remedies for our various illnesses and injuries. "I think you know pretty well about babies being born, but please read all it says in here about what must be done at the time when the baby comes."

I read while Mother heated the kettle for tea. She brought two steaming cups to the table and a loop of cotton string. "The umbilical cord must be cut to free the baby so he can live his own life. If we're here all alone, you will have to do it. Let's practice."

I gulped. My trembling fingers tied and retied the string around one of Mother's fingers until I could do it very fast without fumbling. Mother set aside a clean string and cloths in preparation, and I read the instructions again and again until the time came for Verna and me to do the chores.

Verna and I bundled up and went out to the chicken house. The wind had died down, and moist, heavy snowflakes fell thick and fast. Silent and relentless, it shut us off from our neighbors. On a clear day, we could see the number forty-three train running along the valley floor. Today, we only heard its muffled whistle and wondered if Father was aboard. We returned to the house with enough coal for the night, hoping to hear that Father had called from the station.

He hadn't.

"Shall I try to do the milking?" I asked. I knew that Father would not be home until the next morning, and the cows had to be milked before then.

"No, I can do it," said Mother who then sighed. "Let's wait awhile until I get this sewing finished. It's not very late yet."

Mother bundled up to go milk Brindle and Cherry. I stood in the doorway, watching her head for the barn, worried for her safety. She yelped, and I ran to her. In an instant, Father emerged like an apparition from behind the curtain of falling snow.

That night I lay next to Verna, unable to sleep. My heart ached with loneliness for Bessie. I said my prayers and cried into my pillow. It was hard to understand God's goodness when he had taken away my sister. At last, I fell into a fitful sleep.

Sometime during the night, a light streaming from the front room woke me. I heard Father nearby.

"I hate to get you out on a night like this, Doctor, but her time has come. Will you please bring Mrs. Stalford with you? I'll call her and tell her to be ready."

I bolted upright. "The baby was coming!" I rifled through the instructions in my head. What to do first?

Father turned from the telephone and saw that I was awake. "There's no need for you to get up, Lenna."

"But I promised Mama I would help," I said in a loud whisper.

"There's nothing to do just now. Dr. Thompson and Mrs. Stalford will be here soon. You can help by not waking Verna and Roy. Just stay in bed like a good girl."

Father treated me as if I were still a little girl, when Mother had told me how much she would rely on me. "There must be hot water," I said, throwing back the quilts and searching for my slippers. "The doctor book said so."

"Get back in bed, Lenna. I'll stir up the fire and put the kettle on."

Surely he didn't expect me to sleep at a time like this! I lay back down and listened to the fire crackling and then the water bubbling. I longed for Verna's company in the darkness, but dared not wake her. I startled when Mother sent out a loud moan, and I stared at the strip of light peaking out from under the door to their room.

"Please, God, don't let it hurt my mother too much," I prayed.

I must have dropped off to sleep, because I awoke again, this time to Father holding the lamp and leading the doctor and Mrs. Stalford past my door. Shame pressed down on my chest when I realized I'd abandoned by post. I'd fallen asleep while mother suffered in the next room.

"Oh! Oh! Joe!" she cried out. Then a new sound, sharp and high pitched.

The doctor laughed. "With lungs like that, there can't be much wrong with this young lady." The baby! Hugging my knees, I rocked back and forth.

Excitement turned into worry when the baby kept on crying. It took quite some time before I realized why the sound was so loud. Roy was sitting up on the cot, bellowing. So focused on hearing every sound in the next room, my mind hadn't registered the source. I flew out of bed, took him in my arms, and comforted him as best I could. My heart sank at the thought that I had failed Mother again, and I began to cry right along with him. I longed for Bessie to help me. My tears mingled with Roy's as he wailed and sobbed against my neck.

"Well, look at you two," Mrs. Stalford said. "Lenna, what are you crying about?

You have a beautiful baby sister. Now do you suppose you can get that young man back to sleep? I'm going to be pretty busy for awhile."

"Then may I see Mother and the baby?" I said, rubbing away the tears.

"Do you suppose you could wait until morning? Your mother's fine. She's just very tired. You could help best by getting lots of sleep so you can help me tomorrow."

Mother had told me to help anyway I could. If this was the way, I'd do it. I soon had Roy back to sleep, and I crept into bed beside Verna.

The ringing telephone woke me in the dark. I heard Father talking to Dr. Thompson, then Mrs. Disbrow. He told her Mrs. Stalford must go into town for a premature birth and could she come out and help with the baby. I jumped out of bed, eager to help.

Father and Mrs. Stalford stood by the door, buttoning their coats. "I have to take Mrs. Stalford into town, Lenna. You're in charge until Mrs. Disbrow gets here. Should be any time now."

Verna came wandering into the kitchen, sleepy eyed, and Mrs. Stalford told her about the new baby. After she stole my thunder, I was especially glad she was leaving. At last, I could take charge of the house and redeem myself in Mother's eyes.

Verna and I were doing the dishes when Mrs. Disbrow arrived. She swept right past us to Mother and the baby. "Well, look what we have here! Fine time you picked to come into the world, young lady! There's a blizzard blowing up!"

In no time at all, she had Mother's bed changed and the room straightened up. She told us to answer the telephone and take care of Roy. Word of the baby spread fast over the party line. Calls from our neighbors kept us busy, but we found plenty of excuses to go in and peek at our new baby sister.

Father called at ten o'clock and said he wouldn't be home soon. "There's a connecting rod burned out on the car. It may take hours to fix."

The snow came down more heavily as the day wore on. In the afternoon, the wind began to rise. Deep drifts built up between the house and the barn. Jack Disbrow called in the afternoon to say that he would come for his mother soon to avoid driving after dark. Father telephoned that he would not be home until later and asked us to start the chores.

"Bye, girls. You're in charge now," Mrs. Disbrow said as she climbed into Jack's wagon. The trotting team turned out of the yard, swallowed up by the wind-driven snow. I thought of the thread of worry I'd heard in Father's voice and hustled Verna into warm clothes and out the door.

We husked corn for the pig and put bundles of fodder in the mangers for the cows. Duke heard us in the cow shed and whimpered from his stall. I climbed to the loft and threw down hay for the horses. Verna strewed some feed on the floor for the chickens, though they were already asleep on their perches. I felt guilty about not feeding the chickens early enough. We looked for eggs and slipped the few we found into our coat pockets.

Verna and I left the relative warmth of the barn and faced the storm. It was early dusk and in the blinding snow and bitter cold, I longed for Bessie to be here. We fought our way through a waist-deep drift between the barn and the house, where the wind had blown the snow clean from the doorstep.

Mother kept us busy with directions to bring her this or take away that for the baby was awake and needing attention. There was coal to bring in for the night, supper to start, and lamps to light. As dark descended, the phone rang—ten ominous rings.

"Warning to all stockmen. Blizzard conditions will prevail in this area tonight and tomorrow. Take all necessary precautions," the operator said.

Mother tried to keep up our spirits, keeping a cheerful tone in her voice, but I saw the worry in her eyes.

The wind howled and the walls creaked with every cold blast. The chill seeped in around the windows and the door, setting the lamp to flickering. I added more coal to the fire.

"Better bring the bedding I washed from Bessie's bed," said Mother. "We'll need extra covers tonight." But the bedding hadn't dried. It hung frozen stiff on the line in the lean-to.

I found an extra cover for Mother's bed and Verna and I pushed and pulled her bed away from the wall and the window where little pyramids of snow mounded at the inside corners.

I heated up Mrs. Disbrow's soup of root vegetables and beans. The smell of rutabagas and carrots and onions made me hungry, but I pushed the pot to the back of the stove to keep it warm. Verna and I propped our feet up on the oven door and soaked up the heat.

I thought I heard the wind knock against the door with a dull thud. The door swung open and Father burst in, snow swirling around him.

"I never was so glad to be home!"

We were all relieved to have Father home safe, but I also felt a warmth that didn't come from the stove. Rather, it came from knowing that Mother had depended on me, and that I had done a good job.

The next day and the next, the snow and wind whipped our world. The cold grew deeper, and the drifts grew higher by the hour.

Friday morning, we discovered we were out of bread. Bessie's death, Dorothy's birth, and the storm had consumed all our attention, and no one had thought about bread.

"You girls will have to learn how to bake bread sooner or later and it might as well be now," Mother said.

Making the bread took most of the morning. We were so busy measuring, mixing, and kneading, we didn't notice the wind going down. By noon, the snow stopped. The sky grew lighter, and in the silence left by the departing wind, the cold deepened. We scraped the frost off the panes to look out on a blanket of diamonds. The drift before the back door hid the barn to its roof, and the straw stack was a great white mound. Looking down the valley, we saw rounded outlines of people's houses and barns. Nothing moved in the silent world.

Then something knocked against the door. We all looked at each other. I could hardly believe it, but there it was again—a knocking. Father opened it to Dad Jahns, rounder than ever in layers of coats and sweaters. His ears were covered by a brown wool scarf wrapped over his felt hat. He spoke through icicles hanging from his mustache. "Was rubbering in on the phone and heard you was out of bread. Baked you some biscuits." He handed Father a package wrapped in newspaper.

Father looked dumbfounded. It took him a moment before he tried to usher the old man inside. "Come in. Come on in, man. You are a welcome sight."

"Can't. It's a long half mile through them drifts. Some of them are higher than I am. You'll have to warm them biscuits. Took me longer than I expected."

"We do wish you'd come in," Father said.

"I'm so wrapped up it wouldn't pay me to unwrap and wrap up again."

"Aren't you cold?"

"Nope. A man gets heated up shoveling through them drifts. Guess I'll take the pan back with me if you'll take the biscuits off."

I dumped out the biscuits and handed Father the pan.

"We won't forget your kindness," Father said.

"How's the missus and the baby?"

"They're both doing just fine. Thanks for asking."

"Has it got a name?"

That took Father aback, I think. "It's a she. Her name is Dorothy."

Dad Jahns nodded and turned back toward the pasture. "Better get out and do some shoveling yourself," he shouted as he veered to avoid the huge drift between the house and the barn. The old man made no bones about his poor opinion of the preacher trying to be a farmer, only this time cackling laughter floated back to us.

Chapter 26

Mother and the Model T

Mother in the Model T

Dorothy was two years old when Mother decided she must learn to drive the Model T. Our world had changed considerably since that spring blizzard of 1917. The US had entered the war in April, and Father took advantage of higher demand and prices for wheat and beef. He'd taken a loan for more machinery and cattle, and he'd purchased two draft horses, Babe and Bet. The farm work took all his time, and he quit preaching altogether. His health was good, so Mother didn't worry about him anymore. We all felt settled and happy on our prairie homestead, but Mother wanted the freedom and convenience of a quicker trip into town. She asked Father several times, and he came up with one excuse after another to avoid teaching her how to drive.

Father knew Mother had no knack with machinery. She regarded it as a personal affront when any contraption dared to do less than it was built to do. Her sewing machine drove her to despair. She fought it bitterly until it worked right again, but usually it didn't get back to normal until Father made the repair or adjustment. Mother could solve most of our problems—unless they had to do with machinery.

One morning after a heavy shower had washed down the dust and made things too wet for Father to do his usual farm work, Mother came out to the barn where I was helping Father organize his tools. She asked him once again to teach her to drive the car.

"Oh, Dearie, why today? There are so many little jobs I want to get done around here. Besides, it's too muddy. Some other day we'll do it."

"I'm tired of your excuses." She crossed her arms and her eyebrows, which made her look extremely determined. "It's not really muddy, and those jobs can wait. It's a nice cool morning and you have time."

Father didn't look convinced. He gathered up a pile of nails and dropped them in a tin can, avoiding her sharp gaze.

"Joe, I want to learn today. If you won't teach me, I'll just teach myself. Where's that automobile instruction book?" she said as she headed out of the barn.

Father knew he was licked.

He backed the car out of the garage, put the folding top down, and fastened the cover over it. Father was proud of the car. Not many people in the valley had automobiles, and he had heard the grumblings of some about our family's extravagance. Mother had given such gossip little attention. "We needed it; we need it now. Let them talk." She had a way of cutting through problems with a few well-chosen words that didn't always solve the problem, and sometimes she hurt people's feelings, but her position was always clear. Father cleaned the windshield and headlights. He'd gotten over any guilt he might have had and took great pride in the car, keeping it clean and well maintained.

Mother came out of the house wearing her sunbonnet. Sunbonnets had long been out of style, but the sun burned hot on the South Dakota prairie. Grandma made brown-and-white checked ones for each of us, and Mother wore hers whenever she worked outdoors. Verna and I were well aware of how old fashioned they were and wore them only when she insisted.

"I left the motor running, for even if you learn to drive the car, you must not try to crank it. Dad Jahns told me yesterday that Ron broke his arm cranking his Ford last week," Father warned.

Mother climbed into the driver's seat, and the car motor promptly died.

"Well, you may as well know how to set the gas and spark so it will start," Father said. "Put the spark lever about there, and pull the gas down to here." It seemed to me, as I watched from the doorstep, that this information was entirely unnecessary. Mother or Verna or I always sat in the front seat to advance or set the spark and gas levers for him when he started the car.

He stepped down from the running board and went around in front to crank the motor. He cranked and cranked and nothing happened. "Advance the spark a little. Advance the gas." His voice rose a little. "You must have put it down too far. Reset the spark. More!"

Breathless from cranking, he came back to look at the controls. "It has to go. It was working all right a few minutes ago." He readjusted the lever. Paused. Looked up at Mother. "Woman, you have the magneto off!"

Verna and I were shocked to hear Father speak so sharply to Mother. He was seldom cross with any of us.

"Do just what I tell you to do after this."

We knew Mother was off to a very bad start in her driving lesson.

Father cranked it again, and this time the motor started. Father stood on the running board beside Mother and instructed her. "First release the emergency brake here on the left." Mother leaned down and released it.

"Now step on the low pedal, advance the gas lever a little, and take your right foot off the brake pedal."

Mother just looked at him and didn't make a move.

"As the car goes forward in low speed, gradually lift your left foot off the low pedal, and you'll be in high. Then all you have to do is adjust the gas lever to the speed you wish to travel."

"I'm afraid I'll hit something here in the yard," Mother said, not making any attempt to follow his instructions. "Why can't we go across the road? Out there on the sod there wouldn't be any danger."

"All right. Move over," Father said gruffly. He drove through the gate, across the road, and out onto the prairie grass. I carried Roy, and Verna and I walked as far as the gate to watch.

"I'll stand here on the running board. Show me now how you'd start the car forward," Father said.

Mother moved back into the driver's seat. We could hear her repeating Father's instructions to herself: "Release the hand brake, press on the low pedal, advance the gas."

The car started forward with a jerk that sent Father sprawling on the wet grass.

"Oh, Joe!" Mother took off across the prairie.

Father scrambled to his feet and cupped his hands. "Turn off the gas," he shouted. "Pull the hand brake." His voice trailed off. "Turn off the magneto," he said in a hoarse whimper. Mother was already too far gone.

Father held his head in despair. "Why did I let her drive? She'll kill herself."

Mother and the car bounced over sagebrush up the incline toward the Roberts place. She didn't slow down, even going uphill. The car disappeared over the rise then came in sight when she climbed the next one.

Father turned to see us standing there wide-eyed with fear. He ordered us into the house, but we didn't budge. We kept our eyes on Mother, appearing and disappearing, she and the Model T growing smaller with each sighting. She was heading for the water holes and a gully washed out by spring floods.

"Go back to the house, I said!"

I had never seen Father so upset. Roy started crying at the sound of his angry voice. We hurried to the house and stood at the door. I jiggled Roy gently to soothe him, as we watched Mother tear across the land, heading straight for the yard. Her sunbonnet had blown off her head but remained tied under her chin, flapping at her back in the wind. She was sitting very straight, clutching the steering wheel as the car bounced along. It must have been going thirty miles an hour. Her hair was blowing back from her face, and sometimes the car bounced so high Mother was lifted right off the seat.

Father waved his hat as though he was trying to head off a herd of rushing cattle. Mother kept on coming, staring straight ahead. As she came nearer, I thought I detected a grin and a look of sheer joy—or terror.

"Push up the gas lever! Up! Step on the brake! Turn the magneto key! Pull the emergency brake!"

Mother hung onto the steering wheel and continued to stare straight ahead. Directly opposite us, the car turned in mid-air at the top of a bounce and continued toward us down the hill. It fairly flew off the wash-out, narrowly missed the water hole, and headed for the gate, where Father stood his ground.

"Turn off the switch! Step on the brake! The brake, the brake! Turn off the gas!"

Mother's catatonic stare broke, no doubt at the sight of Father standing directly in her path. She looked like she was trying to do everything at once. She pulled the hand brake, stepped on the pedals, grabbed at the levers. At last, in the final seconds before disaster, she reached down and turned the magneto switch. Father leapt away as the car rolled past him and stopped just inside the gate.

Mother looked like a pink-cheeked young girl with her hair hanging in loose waves down around her shoulders and her eyes dark and shining.

"Dearie, are you all right?" he said, staggering to her side.

"Of course, I'm all right," she said. "But why did you try to teach me everything at once, and forget to tell me how to stop the thing? It's a good thing I'm smart enough to figure out some things by myself."

Invariably, in any confrontation between Mother and the Model T, the car was the loser. One day the car clattered down the hill, returning from a trip to Piedmont with Mother at the wheel. A front tire bounced and flapped around the axle. The car tipped crazily as the rim of the wheel ground along in the rut of the road.

"This car gets harder to steer every day!" Mother complained as she lifted the groceries from the back seat. When I pointed out the condition of the tire, she said, "I thought something must be wrong, but knew I couldn't do anything about it if I did stop, so I kept on coming."

Another time Mother was on her way home with Roy in the passenger seat. An afternoon cloudburst had washed out a culvert, so she backed the car up and took a run at it. Three leaves in the front spring had to be replaced, and my little brother had a broken collarbone. He bounced so high he struck a crossbar in the folding top of the automobile.

At the end of that summer, Mother decided she should drive the car to take us hunting for wild plums in the eroded gullies of the shale hills distant from our house. There was no discernible trail, but Mother drove right up to the thicket of plum trees. We picked syrup pails full of the purple and red fruit. When it came time to go home, she said backing the car out would be dangerous. She insisted it would be safer if the Model T could leap the deep but narrow gully ahead of us. The engine roared like a wild animal when she revved it, and we held on for our lives. We landed safely on the other side, but the plums flew out of their pails. They rained down on us and a coyote hiding in the gully. He fled, howling across the prairie.

That fall Mother returned one day from a drive to Piedmont and discovered a board had worked its way loose from the bottom of the toolbox. All the automobile tools had fallen out on the road. Verna and I went with Mother to retrace her route. We found tools lying at intervals all along the road, distributed at the rate of about a tool every mile. The jack was lying in the middle of the road just outside Piedmont.

"Guess I was going too fast," Mother admitted. "I did hit one of those big bumps in the hogbacks pretty hard. Something should be done about that road."

In the fifty years that followed, Mother drove thousands of miles. It never got easier for her, but she loved pitting herself against the unwilling machine. Somehow, in spite of everything, she always emerged the winner.

Chapter 27

The Literary Society

I think we need more social life in the valley," Mother said one evening at supper. "When I was a teacher in Nebraska, we had a literary society that met once a month, and everybody in the community came. We had plays, lectures, debates—whatever the program committee came up with, and afterward, we had social time. I think we need something like that here."

Father just kept his head down, sopping up gravy with a hunk of bread.

His lack of enthusiasm didn't stop Mother. In the weeks that followed, she got people together for an organizational meeting, and before the end of it, they'd formed The Valley Literary Society and made plans for a Christmas Eve program.

Father and Mother talked in the kitchen after that first meeting. "This will be good for the whole community," Mother said, flushed with her success. "We need more fun in our lives and opportunities to express ourselves and our talents. Did you notice we had people all the way from Coffee Flats and the Hudson neighborhood?"

"We had a nice time," Father said. "But I didn't like the suggestion to have dancing after the meetings. No good can come from that. And what about this Christmas program they're planning? First thing you know, people will be going to that and not to church."

"No, Joe. If we can get people who can't or won't go to church to celebrate Christmas this way, I think we've done a Christian service. I'm sure this won't interfere with church services or the Sunday school program."

"Well, our girls aren't going to a dance," Father said.

"We could leave before the dancing started. And why cross your bridges? They just mentioned dancing. They didn't definitely decide to have it."

After we children were supposed to be asleep, I heard them continue talking about it, and I sensed the tension between them.

"I don't think we need more social life, as you call it," Father said. "We have our work, our home, good books, our friends, and our church. What more do we need? I wish you'd never started this literary society business."

"You're different from most people. You can be content with staying home most of the time, but I like the companionship and the chance to express my ideas and hear those of others. I think most people do, and you do more than you realize. Our girls need more social experience too. The whole community needs it."

Father exploded. "Social experience! Having our girls stared at by rough and tough cowboys and learning bad manners and language is the social experience they'll have. First thing you know, they'll be marrying one of those cowboys."

Mother sounded as angry as he did. "Don't be ridiculous. Most of the children of this community come from God-fearing homes. And maybe we can teach them better manners through an organization like this. Sometimes I don't understand you at all, making such a big thing out of plans for a monthly get-together."

I lay wide awake for a long time after they went to bed, thinking about what Father had said. Marrying a cowboy hadn't entered my mind until he brought it up. The only cowboys I knew were the Sawyer brothers, Walter Huff, Larry Harder, and Jim Hopper. All the boys at school wanted to be cowboys, but it was the young men out of school for several years who rode the broncos at the rodeos and wore chaps, spurs, and ten-gallon hats wherever they went. Why did Father think it would be so wrong to marry a cowboy? Everybody else seemed to think they were special.

The night of the literary society's Christmas program was a bitter, cold one. A thick cover of snow crunched underfoot and gleamed under a full yellow moon. Adolph had gone home to Yankton for Christmas and Tom McPherson had pitched in, helping Father haul hay and cut ice in the water holes for the cattle and horses.

"I just can't go to that thing tonight," Father said at supper. "I'm worn out, my leg aches, and I think I'm getting a cold. I'll stay home with the little ones. You go ahead."

"Oh, Papa, please go," Verna said. "I want you to hear me say my poem."

"I'd better not, my girl. You'll do well, I know."

Mother didn't complain, but she bowed her head and didn't look anymore at Father. She cheered up some when Tom said he'd ride along with us.

As we drove into the schoolyard, Mr. Disbrow came running toward us from the store.

"Jim Hopper's had a runaway and is badly hurt. We've got to have help," he shouted.

"Go see what can be done, Tom," Mother said. "We'll stay here at the school."

We were hardly inside the schoolroom when Edna and Ruby Hopper appeared in the doorway, their cheeks red and wet from crying. People pressed around them, and word went round that Jim had a broken leg and injured back. The spring wagon was smashed, but somehow, the girls weren't hurt.

Tom strode over to Mother. "We've got to get Jim to the doctor in Edgemont. Should I take the car?"

"Of course," she said.

It took a while to settle the crowd, but eventually, the Christmas program got underway. I had been asked to read the Christmas story from the Bible. It hadn't occurred to Mother to have me practice reading it aloud, and when I came to the part about the wise men offering incense and myrrh to the Christ child, I read "incense and Myra," which brought titters from Myra Johnson and her family. I blushed with embarrassment and struggled to get through the rest.

After the program, refreshments were served. Mother, as usual, got so interested in talking to people that she was still eating her cake when Walter Hunt and some of the other boys started moving chairs and desks back along the walls.

"Sorry to ask you to move, but we can't dance until the floor is cleared," Walter said.

Mother swallowed her cake in one big bite and looked anxiously toward the door. She hadn't expected the dancing and her eyes searched for Tom among the young people clustered around the door. Though she turned back to talk to the other women, she looked trapped, and her gaze kept returning to the door, surely hoping Tom would rescue us from the dance.

Mr. Soley tuned up his fiddle and Mrs. Cass started playing chords on the organ. Soon the floor crowded with people, young and old, graceful and not so graceful, dancing to "Ain't We Got Fun," a familiar tune I recognized right off. Adolph had given us the sheet music the week before, and we had already learned to play it.

Verna and I watched wide-eyed. We had never seen people dance before. We knew it must be wicked, because Father insisted it was, and Mother had never disagreed. Everyone was having such a good time; it was hard to believe it could be so bad.

At the end of the first dance, Mother called me over. "Please get our coats so we'll be ready to go when Tom comes. He'll surely be along soon."

I could tell that Mother was anxious, but under her worried brows, I detected a twinkle in her eyes.

Mr. Soley walked across the floor to Mother, his fiddle under his arm. "I'm going to pass the fiddle on to John here, if you'll pleasure me with a dance."

The room quieted and heads turned toward Mother.

She blushed and hesitated, looking confused. It took her a few seconds to lift her chin and look at Mr. Soley. "No, thank you," she said, smiling politely. "I don't dance. The girls and I are just waiting for Tom. We'll be going home soon."

Mr. Soley bowed a little and smiled, lifted the violin to his shoulder and fiddled his way back to the other side of the room.

"At least they all know why we are still here," said Mother, more to herself than to me.

Soon after, Tom appeared, and we left the lights and the shrill violin and went out into the peaceful, white night.

"I took Jim on home. The doctor put a cast on his leg and said he'd have a bad back for awhile and must stay in bed for a week at least. Sorry to be so late getting back."

"I'm glad you took care of Jim," Mother said, but she wasn't her usual talkative self.

We reached the top of the hill just out of Provo when we heard a strange scraping noise coming from the back. Tom stopped the car and got out to look.

"Something's wrong with this right rear fender. It's hanging down and banging against the tire." He tried to push it back in place, but the fender wouldn't stay.

"Well, this has been a night," Mother said, climbing out to have a look.

"Can't go on with it hanging like this," Tom said. "It would ruin the tire and maybe wreck us. Maybe I can pound it on with a hammer."

Verna and I got out so Tom could get at the tools under the back seat, but no amount of pounding would make the fender stay up.

"Guess I'll have to go back to the schoolhouse and see if I can find help. If I can get the fender off, we can go on home."

Mother and Verna and I climbed back into the cold car, and Tom strode down the road toward the schoolhouse. The moon cast a shadow behind him that looked like an animated telephone pole—long and skinny. We'd all grown fond of him in a short time. He had followed the wheat harvests north from Kansas and stayed in Provo at the end of the season doing odd jobs. Everybody liked him. He was a good worker, and he had a dry wit that kept us entertained. When he smiled, a gold tooth gleamed—army gold, he called it.

"I think Mr. Soley asked me to dance just to embarrass me," mused Mother, more to herself than to us. "He knows well enough that Papa and I are against dancing. I don't think he was being mean, though. He was just teasing me."

"Wasn't that funny when everybody hopped around and wiggled so?" Verna said. "Marcie Cass called it the Camel Walk." We giggled. "All I could think of was mosquito wrigglers in the rain barrel."

Mother laughed with us and said, "Well, Papa was right. We'll probably be criticized for being at the dance. People expect the minister's family to be above such things. But we couldn't help it, and reasonable folks will know that."

"Everybody was having fun," I said. "I don't understand why people think dancing is so terrible."

"It's not the dancing," Mother said. "It's what goes with it that is bad. Careless and evil people spoil it for others. The Bible says, 'Avoid the appearance of evil,' and that's what we must do." An emphatic nod closed the subject.

Tom returned with Andy Sawyer on horseback. The two young men tried tying up the fender with Andy's rope, but that didn't work. They gave up on that and lassoed the whole car, holding the fender away from the tire. Andy wrapped the end of the rope around his saddle horn, and Tom got in and started the car.

Andy rode alongside us, tightening the rope now and then to stop the fender's jiggling.

"He didn't have those furry chaps on at the schoolhouse," Verna said.

"I'll bet they help keep him warm."

"He's a real cowboy," Verna whispered to me, knowing that Mother wouldn't approve of her tone of admiration.

I wondered if he was "rough and tough" as Father had said, and if Father would change his attitude toward cowboys now that this one had been so nice to us. I didn't dare say that out loud.

"It hasn't seemed like Christmas tonight, except for the program," I said, wanting to get Verna off the subject. "But it looks Christmasy. The snow is shining like sugar."

Mother broke into song. "It came upon a midnight clear . . . ." She turned to song whenever time lagged or spirits sagged. We joined in, singing gaily in the quiet night. The coyotes and the jackrabbits must have been surprised at the joyous Christmas carol that rang out over the glittering prairie. In the bright moonlight, we could see the dark buildings of the homesteads all down the valley.

At last we spied the warm beam from the lamp Father left burning for us. In the yard, Andy retrieved his lasso from the sagging fender and loped off down the section line toward home. "Merry Christmas!" he called. By then, it was nearly midnight. His cheer made us smile as it echoed down the still valley.

Chapter 28

Going to School

(left to right) Verna and Lenna O'Neill

In the spring of 1919, when I was eleven years old and Verna was ten, Mother decided we should go to school in Provo. We had never been to a real school, and neither Verna nor I had any interest in leaving our cozy home and the kitchen table where we did our lessons. Nevertheless, Mother and Father thought we should give it a try for the few months that were left before the summer break.

The week before we were to begin, there was a flurry of sewing. Mother made us new jumpers and white blouses on her sewing machine. She even bought us new shoes, which got broken in on the first two-and-one-half-mile trek to the school.

There was cold dew on the short spring grass as we started across the pasture, but the sun was shining, and we knew exactly which hill in the distance we should go over to find Provo. We had watched Old Man Jahns and his snake stick go out of sight over that hill many times as he went to town to get the mail. Our braids were tight and smooth, caught behind our ears with bright new hair ribbons to match the pink and blue jumpers. We put our lunch buckets and tablets down carefully and held our coats snugly around us as we crawled through the barbed-wire fence at the edge of the Spicer land.

"Watch out for the cactus," I said. This morning, especially, I felt the responsibility of being older. Mother had reminded me when she kissed me goodbye.

We crossed the draw and passed the Clemens place. They proved up on their land and had gone back east, leaving their house deserted. Most of the windows were broken, leaving black holes that looked like lonely and desolate skull's eyes.

When we climbed out of the draw, the land became scrubby with sagebrush and bright-green cactus. Greasewood spikes poked up from the ground like traps laying in wait for our new shoes. The washes and gullies we crossed coated them with a layer of dust. A gaggle of sage hens scuttled low between the sagebrush clumps that sent up their heady scent.

After one more rise, we looked down at Provo and the schoolhouse where Father had preached and where we attended services every other Sunday. From our high perch, we could see the children in the yard and hear their squeals of laughter as they played.

"I don't want to go," Verna said.

"I don't either. But Mother said we must."

We clutched our tablets and lunch buckets and slowly walked down the hill. I felt shivery and frightened, but Mother had said that the Cass children and Wilbur Johnson would be there, and the Soleys, and the Hoppers—all the children that went to Sunday school and church with us.

Walking slower than we had on the prairie, we crossed the road. I surveyed the unfenced schoolyard, the shed where the riding horses were tied, the two privies, and the white clapboard schoolhouse. The children stopped their play and watched us. Dotty and Marcie Cass ran out to meet us. Until then, I'd wanted to turn and run.

"You're almost late," Dotty said. "We thought maybe you weren't going to come after all. We've been watching a long time."

A pale, white-haired lady appeared in the doorway. Her old-fashioned high, white-lace collar propped up a sharp chin. Miss Schreckingosht shook a brass bell, and all the children streamed up the steps. Dotty took my hand and pulled me along. Verna disappeared in the crowd.

The familiar room looked different on a school day. Instead of ladies in church hats and men in their Sunday best, sixteen children occupied the rows of desks, which graduated in size to accommodate the little first graders and the big kids in eighth.

The aroma of burning wood from the big stove in the center of the room warmed me with memories of Sunday church services. Though it was spring in the valley, the teacher still had to build a fire to take away the chill.

I watched everyone hang up their coats on a long row of hooks and scramble to take their seats.

"There's no hook left for me," I said.

"Shh. Here's one," Dotty said. "You mustn't talk out loud."

"Lenna, you sit here with Dotty, and Verna, you sit with Edna," Miss Schreckingosht said with a pinched, high-pitched voice. I thought of Mother back home probably singing a happy tune to Dorothy and Roy.

I slid in beside Dotty at one of the double desks along the south side of the room. I was glad that we were so close to the window. We could look out at the store and see the activity in town. I slipped my tablet and pencil into the space beneath the marred desktop, and following Dotty's lead, folded my hands. The teacher stepped up to her platform, sat down at her desk, opened a book, and began to read a story to us.

I glanced to my left and right at the other children, trying not to move my head. I wondered what I had done with my lunch bucket in all the rush and saw that someone had put it on the shelf above the coats in the entry way. Everyone seemed friendly. Going to school wasn't so bad after all, I thought.

Eric Cass, Dotty's brother, sat alone at the desk in front of us. He extended his arm along the back of his bench—which was the front of our desk—and jiggled the top of my glass inkwell, all the while keeping his eyes fixed on Miss Schreckingosht's face, pretending deep absorption in the story. I blushed at the attention.

Miss Schreckingosht droned on, and I felt almost sick with excitement and shyness, but I watched and listened carefully as Mother had told me to do. When she finished reading, she gave me my assignments for the morning. I read in the reader, studied geography and spelling, and worked the arithmetic problems.

At recess, the children surrounded us, all trying to get acquainted, and by noon, my mouth was no longer dry with anxiety. I visited with Dotty and Marcie and the other girls as we ate our lunches and watched the boys tease Verna. They had already discovered the fun in making her big eyes snap and her cheeks blush at their remarks. I was glad when Eric told them to stop.

After the noon recess, Miss Schreckingosht played the organ and we sang "Marching Through Georgia" and "South Dakota Is the Sunshine State." I was surprised that so many of the children didn't sing well. It had never occurred to me that this wasn't an ability shared by everyone.

"Seventh-grade reading class, please come forward. Lenna, you come too." I thought how pleased Mother would be that the teacher had placed me with the advanced readers. Even so, I wasn't sure I liked Miss Schreckingosht. Though she treated us kindly, most of the time her eyes didn't seem to see us at all. When she handed my arithmetic back, I saw that I hadn't fared so well. I'd done almost half the problems wrong, and everybody knew it. I had discovered the first problem with going to school in one room with the other children.

"Do them again, Lenna," said Miss Schreckingosht. "Hand them in before recess." When I finished, I listened to her talk to the eighth graders about Red Cloud and Sitting Bull. I couldn't wait to learn more about those famous Indian fighters. By the end of my first day, I thought I might like school very much.

When dismissal time came, Verna and I said hasty goodbyes and hurried back up the hill. I had my arithmetic book tucked under my arm, and vowed I'd win out over those problems. We ran from the top of the rise until we were out of breath. Then we rested on a flat rock and, seeing our home in the distance, ran again.

Chapter 29

The Killer Blizzard

Rain swept across the prairies on a rising wind. Verna and I were driving the cattle, but it became more and more difficult to keep the cows headed toward home. The rain turned to sleet, and the air grew colder. The cows turned their tails to the wind and refused to move forward. We waved our arms, we shouted, we ran beside them, but no matter how often we turned them toward home, they soon swung back toward the east.

We were returning home from our second day at school. Father had asked us in the morning to bring the cows in on our way back in the afternoon. The storm had come upon us without warning.

"If only Fanny were here to help," I cried. Our herd dog Fanny was a border collie from a line of prizewinning cattle and sheep dogs.

The sleet and cold cut against my face. I could barely see for the rain in my eyes. We had just gotten the cows moving in the right direction again when my heart sank. They had reached the line fence between the Spicer land and the Cavinders'.

"Get along there, you old things!" Verna shouted, trying to move them along the fence.

We ran back and forth, imitating Fanny's herding techniques, but the cows huddled against the fence and ignored us.

"You try to keep them moving when I get them started," I said. "I'm going to crawl through the fence and scare them back away from it."

The sleet turned to thick, wet snow. I crawled under the barbed wire at a spot where the grass seemed firm. I ran along my side of the fence screaming and waving my arms at the cows. They turned and went a few steps, then crowded back to the fence. Again and again, they moved a few feet before returning to the fence.

I kept on with my histrionic herding. The wind that had tossed snow at us in massive swirls died down. It looked like the worst of the storm had passed, and the cattle began to move along. Without the wind, the snow fell like an opaque curtaining dropping before us. It clung to the fence, blanketed the cows' backs, and covered Verna's hair and crusted her eyelashes. We were both wet through and shivering. We had no mittens, and our new shoes were ruined.

Great clots of snow blinded us, but I knew if we followed the fence, it would lead us home. I refused to cry. I was trapped on Cavinder's side of the fence as long as the cows needed prodding away from it and on down the valley. Like the cows, Verna and I lowered our heads and trudged along.

If I had been looking where I was going, and if I could have seen through the sheet of snow, I would have seen the gigantic red and white beast before I nearly walked into it.

I was face to face with Cavinder's bull.

This creature had a penchant for breaking down fences and making a nuisance of himself with bellowing and pawing and malevolent glares. Father would not let us go for the cows if he was anywhere in sight. His bulging, red-rimmed eyes stared at me; they were not blinking and neither were mine.

I got a close look at the snow clinging to his long, bristly eyelashes and the curly mat of red hair between his horns. He lowered his head and continued to stare at me. Then he let out a horrendous snort.

I dove for the fence and rolled under. Facing a forest of legs moving in all directions, I crawled under the cows' bellies and scrambled to my feet. At the sound of the bull, the cows took off running. Verna shouted at them from behind. I ran too and didn't look back until I saw the brace and post at the corner of Cavinder's land. I couldn't see the bull, but I heard the muffled sound of his hoofs—running away from me!

My teeth were chattering and I ached from the cold. When I caught up with Verna, she began to cry.

"Do you think we'll ever get home with these old cows?" she said, her words choppy with shivering.

"Oh, sure," I said, trying to sound more confident than I was. "All we have to do is follow this fence to the drop gate, and then we're practically home."

Before we got to the drop gate, we heard Father calling to us and Fanny barking. Together, the four of us drove the cows home, and we two bedraggled, wet girls fell into the house where Mother and a warm stove were waiting.

The wind built the storm into a howling blizzard that night. For two days, the wind hurled drifts across the land. Hundreds of cattle died during the storm in the valley. They ran from it in fright, piled up in the sheltered ravines and smothered to death. We lost three heifers and a calf from our small herd.

Floods followed the storm. Old Mr. and Mrs. Darby and their hired man were drowned when a wall of water from a broken dam swept over them as they drove their Ford across a gully. Every horse and rider in the valley was bone tired from the three-day search for the victims.

As suddenly as the storm came on, it passed away. The water receded and soaked the prairie. We returned to school the following Friday. At the end of the school term, our report cards said I had passed from sixth to seventh and Verna from fifth to sixth grade. I didn't learn much in that school, but my memories are crowded with the things I learned walking to and from school.

The storm had been a trial that Verna and I endured together. The reward of all that water was a spring to remember. Each walk to school and back gave up gifts of the earth. I cherished the fragrance of the yellow sweet peas we brought home to Mother, the cries and stumblings of the killdeer feigning injury to lead us from its nest, the trembling of the camouflaged horn toad's throat as we discovered it stone still on the hardpan, the frightening sound of the rattlesnake on the ledges at the top of the draw. I can still see the glistening dew caught on the lip of a sago lily and the ants on the waxy sweet hearts of the red and yellow cactus blossoms. One day an albino sage hen preened in the midst of the covey, bowing and walking with proud deliberate steps like a queen strolling among her subjects. I will never forget the sheer joy of buttering fresh-baked bread and swigging it down with cool milk when we got home at the end of the school day. I will always remember the snowflakes catching on the eyelashes of Cavinder's bull

Chapter 30

Prairie Baby

That summer after the killer blizzard, I spent most of my days on the open range watching over the cattle. One afternoon I was reading a book while the cattle grazed, as I did most days. I had tipped my big straw hat to shade my eyes, and I was laying on the prairie grass, my heavy braids coiled into a pillow. Out here Mother couldn't voice her disapproval of *The Adventures of Baron Munchausen*, which I was reading again. What a delightful liar he was! Through half-closed eyes, I watched the bank of clouds grow darker above the northwestern horizon. They'd been building all morning, and I smelled the promise of rain in the air.

Father often sent me out to watch over our herd of sixty-one cattle on rangeland he'd rented beyond the homestead. I was seldom more than a mile or two from home. Astride Duke, I slowly drifting with the grazing cattle or stretched out in the grass reading. Every now and then, I had to ride to cut off an ambitious heifer headed for the Bushnell's cornfield or the Fletcher's wheat.

Fanny always came along to help me keep the strays in check. Father surprised us with her one day, and Mother protested that three dogs were too many.

"We need a good cattle dog," he said. "You know Queen and Prince are not much good at that." To ease the transition, we sent Queen and her pup, Prince, to stay at the Stalfords until Fanny got through the puppy stage. But the Stalfords misunderstood, and when we were ready to take her back, they were unhappy. Elsie cried and Mr. Stalford was angry, so we gave in and let them keep her.

Now Fanny was my faithful sidekick, alert when I drifted off into the baron's tales. She kept raising her head, keeping an eye on the cattle. They were restless and bent on heading in all directions for relief from the early summer heat. I squinted at the sky, trying to calculate the time, but clouds covered the sun.

Though Father had taught me to tell time by the sun, Mother insisted I take a clock along. She wanted to be sure I got the cows back in time for milking. The clock was tied to the saddle, but I felt too lazy to get up and check it.

The next time I looked up from my book, thunderheads were forming. Long, slanting, gray rays swept from the clouds to the darkening horizon. The distant mutter of thunder broke the silence. I scrambled up and stuffed the book into my saddlebag. Duke stood switching away the flies with his long, glossy tail. He never wandered far as long as the bridle reins trailed the ground.

I checked the time. It was half past four—much later than I thought. "Steady, Duke." I tightened the saddle girth and gathered the reins. When I mounted, Duke lifted his head and trotted briskly toward the herd. The air grew still. Lightning flickered to the west, died, and flashed again.

The cattle were strung out over a wide area. Some lay chewing their cud on a hillside not far away, but others had followed the draws and were scattered in small groups almost out of sight. Fanny ran along beside Duke and me as we rode the sagebrush-dotted edge of the draws, searching the rocky sides for strays and looking especially for Brindle, the leader of the herd, due to calve any day now.

The thunder rolled more often, and the sky darkened as I rode. A yellow grayness in the rolling upper clouds promised hail. I urged Duke into a lope. My straw hat slipped off my head and hung by its ties, flapping against my shoulders.

"We've got to hustle." My heels clicked against Duke's belly. "Hee-yaw!"

Fanny herded eight or ten white-faced steers and two cows down the slope toward the others on the hillside. A breeze replaced the sultry air, and a dark wall of rain moved steadily across the prairie. Lightning raced along the clouds, and the thunder grumbled without relief.

The breeze stiffened into wind. I had to unite the herd. There were plenty of settlers' tales about cattle scattered and lost in wind and driving rain. I couldn't let that happen. Duke, Fanny, and I worked swiftly to round up the stragglers before Duke and I turned up the draw for the other cattle.

That's when the storm broke. Hailstones beat against us and rain soaked us through in an instant. Duke refused to go on. He pulled against the reins, turned his back to the wind, and put his head down. I dismounted and led Duke to shelter under a jutting rock. Fanny and I scrunched up and huddled further back under the ledge.

The ground whitened with hailstones. The rain poured over the rock like a waterfall. Tall grass lay flat as the water washed down the slopes. A muddy stream rushed along the valley floor just beyond our feet where minutes before there had been only dusty grass.

I noticed something glistening in the huge boulder supporting the overhang and squeezed closer. A crack in the rock revealed glittering crystals that hung down and formed a fairy palace. Through the slit I saw a mouse's nest shaped to fit between the hanging jewels and the heaps of diamond-like cubes. In the midst of the deluge, I began weaving a story about this little gray king in his crystal palace.

A tug on the reins jerked me back to reality. The hail had stopped and the rain was lightening. Restless in his cramped position, Duke tried to back out from under the rock. Fanny rose and shook herself.

"Hey, you! I'm wet enough!"

I backed Duke out. Most of the saddle had been sheltered from the storm, but the pungent smell of wet horsehair and leather rose up as I mounted. The rain ended, and a low sun broke through the clouds. Mounds of hail were piled in sheltered spots. The storm finished with my part of the world, rumbled off to the southeast.

Duke jogged over the slippery sod. A group of cows were sauntering home about a half mile ahead. I counted and recounted them as they moved. Each time I was one short of the sixty-one cattle I knew I should have.

As I reached the herd, Fanny began to wave back and forth, nipping a lagging heel here and barking at a stubborn head there, relentlessly driving them on. I searched the herd, trying to figure out which one was missing. Father's voice echoed in my mind. "Watch out for Brindle. She's late having her calf and is slow and clumsy these days."

Brindle was the missing cow.

Dusk was deepening. "Take them home, Fanny." She hesitated to leave me. "Go on. Take them home, girl!" She started off, glanced back at me, and then trotted after the cattle moving homeward.

I wheeled Duke about knowing I would have to retrace the wanderings of the herd as it had leisurely grazed that day. Duke couldn't go fast on the wet prairie. Places that had been sunbaked before—so arid and alkaline that even grass would not grow in them—were now slippery, treacherous gumbo.

The uplands, from which I had just brought the herd, had a thousand places where a cow lying down could be completely hidden. My eyes searched every ridge, every draw. Night was drawing in. I trusted Duke to take care of me. He never failed me. He'd been my companion ever since I was old enough to ride. We understood each other.

Near dark we returned to the place where I had lain in the grass and finished my book. Brindle would not have gone unseen on the hill. She must be in one of the draws, I thought. I led Duke to the nearest ravine, and he began to pick his way down.

Fanny ran up beside us, panting, and though she hadn't done as she had been told, I was glad to see her.

The wind was beginning to blow from the north. A coyote barked in the distance. Another one answered. More coyotes joined in the gregarious yapping and mournful howling. Duke's ears pointed forward. His head rose. He slowed to a near standstill, and then walked warily. I peered into the night trying to see what Duke sensed. The darkness in the draw welled up as if to drown us all as Duke descended into its depths.

My eyes grew accustomed to the dark. In a moment, the sight of Brindle emerged from the shadows. A white-faced calf stood beside her. Brindle bawled and nudged her new baby as we approached, then took several tentative steps away from us, mooed, and nudged it again to lead it away.

"Careful, Fanny. Wait."

I reined in the horse and sat back in the saddle feeling relieved before the knowledge hit that I would have to find a way to get Brindle and her knobby-kneed calf home. A barking coyote at the edge of the draw made my decision. "Take her, Fanny. Take her home," I called, riding beside the cow to head her up out of the ravine. Brindle whirled and bunted at the dog, refusing to leave her calf. I called Fanny off and turned Duke back.

When I approached the cow and calf again, Duke reached out and nipped Brindle's rump. She started up the incline, the clumsy calf following behind. After a few steps, the cow stopped and looked back, calling the calf, and we all stopped to wait for it.

At the top of the draw, the prairie sloped gently away from us in the cool starlight. After the blackness of the draw, the world seemed wonderfully bright. Brindle went along more willingly now. Fanny trotted at her heels, just ahead of Duke and me. Every so often, our caravan came to a halt as the wobbly calf stumbled to its knees or lay down and refused to move. I marveled at its strength, even as it faltered.

In the dark aftermath of the storm, I heard the coyotes' yips, the squeaking of the saddle leather, the cracking sound of the cow's hoofs, and nothing more. Brindle turned again to lick and comfort her baby. Duke tossed his head and paced. Fanny crouched nearby. Tired and hungry, I searched the blackness ahead for the lights of home.

At last, I saw a small beam shining steadily across the wide prairie. I had never returned home after dark. The cow mooed, and I saw the calf crumpled on the sod again, bawling. We waited for the calf to suckle and get strength to go the rest of the way home.

When we resumed our journey, the songs of the frogs rose up from the water hole. As we approached, a startled bird screamed and darted from the shadows, startling all of us. Brindle's feet sucked in and out of the mud when she drank from the silver water. Fanny waded in too, lapped her fill, and scrambled to the rim of the gulch. The calf rested on dry ground. Duke walked to the water's edge, put his head down, and drank.

I relaxed in the saddle and waited. The coyotes' calls no longer struck me as ominous. I inhaled the sage-scented air and felt my love for this land; it was as strong as my love for the faithful animals taking me home and my family waiting where the light glimmered in the distance.

Fanny shattered the quiet with loud, insistent barking. The drumming hoofbeats of a galloping horse rumbled underneath. My heart leapt into my throat. Duke drew back from the water and lifted his ears. The cow hurried to her calf. Fanny returned to my side. I saw the silhouette of a man on a horse on the ridge above the water hole. The rider came to a stop and called out. "Is that you, Lenna?"

Eric Cass had come like a knight on horseback to find me. My heart swelled. From the first day at school in Edgemont, Eric had chosen me, and though I was embarrassed by his attentions, I was proud. The Casses were our very good friends. At first my Irish-to-the-core father felt a bit strained around Fred, who was English, but as time went on, a strong friendship developed between us and the Cass family. At school, we girls had felt that Eric's sister, Dotty, was our very best friend, and though I kept it to myself, I had a warm spot in my heart for Eric.

I called up to him in a small voice. "I've been trying to get this new calf home." I urged Brindle and her calf away from the water hole.

Eric swung his horse, Silver, and trotted to my side. "I better carry that young one the rest of the way, I guess." He was only thirteen but big and strong for his age. He dismounted, put his arms around the calf, and lifted it to the withers of his horse.

"You should have seen your folks when the cows came home without you. Some commotion! Your mom was plenty worried. Your dad too, but he got so riled up trying to catch a horse, he was about wild. I think he was ready to start out on foot when we got there, but my dad said no man in his right mind would try walking through prickly cactus at night." The calf struggled against him. "Help me steady this little critter, will you, while I get on my horse?"

He threw his leg over the saddle and then balanced the calf in front of it. Duke and I followed Eric and Silver toward home, but Brindle stood and bawled for a moment before she hurried after us. I stole a glance at Eric's face shadowed under his wide-brimmed hat. Watching him take charge of getting us home lit a warm glow in my heart. I felt safe and happy riding beside him.

The horses broke into a trot, and Fanny hurried Brindle along. At the corral gate, Father's voice rang out.

"Is that you, Lenna?"

"Yes, Papa. We brought Brindle and her new baby home!"

Chapter 31

Mother Becomes a Teacher

At the end of that summer, when the dry wind had curled the grass blades and we were all limping toward a final break in the heat, a man drove his team and wagon into our yard. I ran down the potato rows in back of the house, holding my skirt close so I wouldn't brush off the Paris Green potato-bug poison Father had sprayed on them the night before. Mother came up from the far end of the garden, where she was hoeing the vegetables that Father had no time to care for.

Mother had "lost her figure," as she referred to her widened hips and belly, after Dorothy's birth. She was wearing baggy Montgomery Ward coveralls that did nothing to help her looks. We always referred to them by the full name, as if, somehow, that made them sound less like men's clothing. In the spring, her skirt had caught on the trip lever of the harrow when she was helping Father prepare a field for planting. She might have been dragged to her death if the horses hadn't responded to her hollering. That very day, she sent the mail order for the Montgomery Ward coveralls, and ever since they arrived, she wore them when she worked, not caring a whit how they looked.

She wiped her red and grimy face with the back of her arm before she extended her hand. "Good morning, Mr. Soley. Mr. O'Neill is helping Mr. Howell this morning. He'll be home at noon."

Mother had a way of taking command of a conversation.

"Well I didn't exactly come to see Mr. O'Neill anyway. I'm on my way over to Scott's and thought I'd stop on the way and talk to you." He twirled the brim of his hat as he talked. "I may as well come right to the point. The school board sent me over to ask if you'd be interested in teaching Provo School this next year."

Mother's eyes widened. "Miss Schreckingosht is not coming back?"

"Well, she's been there a long time, and some of the parents are wanting a change. We know you teach your girls at home and that you used to be a teacher. Thought you might be interested in teaching our kids too."

"When is Miss Schreckingosht leaving?"

"She's already gone." Mr. Soley wiped his forehead with his kerchief and put his hat back on. "School should start in a few weeks, and we need a teacher, Mrs. O'Neill."

"I'll have to talk it over with Mr. O'Neill. I don't really know how we'd manage it."

"Let's say you'll let us know in ten days. School starts the second week in September, right after the fair. We pay forty dollars a month for the eight months."

"I'll let you know."

Mr. Soley started to leave and then turned back. "You're not in the family way, are you? That would make it quite impossible, of course."

Mother gasped and glanced down at her thick waist. "No, Mr. Soley. I am not."

I followed Mother back down through the potato patch. "What does being in the family way mean?"

"It means going to have a baby. No gentleman would say a thing like that to a lady. He probably doesn't know any better. I suppose I do look big as a moose in these." She looked down at her baggy work outfit. "Darn these Montgomery Ward coveralls!"

"I would be so happy teaching," Mother said later as she talked over the prospect with Father. "And we do need the money."

Mother rarely talked about money. It was Father who continued to borrow from the bank for the sake of growing the farm. That summer his dream of turning our modest homestead into a thriving, modern farm had begun to come true. We had more cattle and horses and farm machinery than we'd ever expected, and the Edgemont bank was always willing to let the ex-preacher sign another note.

Mother had her own dreams. She planned and longed for a new house for us. "We can't go on living this way," she had said more than once. "Our children are growing, and they must know something better than this." She had argued that we were too crowded in the makeshift house. "We have to sleep all in one room. Our girls will be young ladies before we know it."

No amount of talk had convinced Father. She never could pin him down to make specific plans. With the teaching job in Provo, she saw the opportunity at last to earn enough money to build her dream house.

"Give me time to think about it," Father said. He finished his dinner quickly and left the house without giving Mother a kiss.

A week later, Mother signed the contract, on condition that Verna and I could attend Provo School tuition free and that she could get a valid certificate. She traveled to Hot Springs at the end of August to take an exam for her license to teach in South Dakota. I never had any doubt that she would pass. My mother was the smartest person I knew.

She bought a dun-colored horse and a buggy to drive back and forth from Provo reasoning it would be more reliable than the car, and it would cost less. The horse was cheap, because it was no longer young, but it had been a woman's driving horse and had a reputation for steadiness and stamina.

Mother and Father decided Verna and I would take turns going to school. One of us always had to stay home to take care of the babies, do household chores, and prepare the meals. Neither of us had an objection to this arrangement. We liked being at home.

So our lives changed again. I helped Father walk the fence on the land he'd acquired with the last loan from the bank. We tightened wires with the wire stretcher, reset posts, and cut a gate to our west pastures. Father was happy with the new land, and Mother was happy organizing for her teaching post and planning the house she knew she'd get built with her earnings.

Chapter 32

Plans

Eighteen children attended the Provo school when Mother began teaching, but as the fall harvest wound down and as Mother's reputation as a good teacher grew, more and more of the older children came. They soon discovered that, with Mother in charge, school could be exciting and fun, and they began to attend regularly. Her reputation was made when she taught fourteen-year-old Wilbur Johnson arithmetic. He applied his new skills to figuring out how much barbed wire his father needed to fence a triangular field. By the end of the first month, five more kids started coming to school.

The job was hard. In addition to teaching, Mother had to keep the schoolroom clean and comfortable. She bought material and made scrim curtains for the lower half of the windows and sent the bill to the school board. At the end of every school day, she swept and dusted the room so it would be ready for the next day. As cool days came on, she went to school earlier so she could light a fire in the base-burner to take the chill off the room before the children arrived.

One crisp September day after school, Mother and I drove down past the depot to a converted boxcar, the home of two of her students. Two young Mexican girls, Viney and

Henrietta Perea, lived there with their father, the railroad section foreman. Viney had been absent from school for many days, and Mother hadn't been able to understand six-year-old Henrietta when she tried to explain her sister's absence in broken English.

I waited in the buggy while Mother went in. Before long, she came out with an armload of clothes. "The girls are going home with us to stay a few days. Their mother is very sick, and the father has enough to do to take care of the baby boy and the sick mother."

At home, I heard Mother tell Father there was no hope for the poor woman, and sure enough, she died four days after the girls came to stay with us. Mother closed school the day of the funeral, drove to the boxcar, dressed the girls and the baby in their best clothes, and took Mr. Perea and his little family to Edgemont. Verna and I went too.

We had never attended a funeral before, but Mother thought our presence might help Viney and Henrietta. We were among the few at the long Catholic service. Viney and Mr. Perea cried, but Henrietta sat stiff and sullen. We filed out to watch the burial in the cemetery behind the chapel, and then returned to the sanctuary. Henrietta refused the holy water the priest offered and kicked him. "My Henrietta, she bad, she wicked!" Mr. Perea said as he marched her out of the church.

Mother hurried after him. "She's afraid, Mr. Perea. Please don't punish her. She's fighting her fear the only way she knows."

Henrietta was fighting all right.

"First I lose my wife. All my money gone to pay the priest. Now Henrietta shame us all." He turned away, sobbing.

Mr. Perea's troubles didn't end there. The next day, as he was getting ready to move to Texas with his children, the police came and accused him of illegally crossing the border from Mexico. The police accompanied the family back to Texas, where presumably they were deported. We never saw Viney or Henrietta again.

We had been very crowded the nights the Perea girls had stayed with us, and that got Mother talking again about the new house. In the course of helping the family, Mother had learned that Mr. Perea earned seventy-five dollars a month working as section foreman.

"Seems strange to me that a railroad section man can earn more in a month than a teacher helping shape the lives of more than twenty children. I'm going to talk to the school board members. I'll not teach for forty dollars."

To her surprise, the salary was raised to seventy-five dollars without any dissent.

"Imagine that!" Mother said. "Must be they knew all along I was being underpaid."

The windfall made Mother more impatient than ever with Father's stubborn refusal to build a new house. "My salary will be coming in regularly, and you have most of the farm machinery you'll ever need. Why don't we at least make some plans? We could build a nice house just west of this one. If things don't work out, we just won't build. Or maybe we can build a part of it each year till it's done."

Mother was relentless, and so, the planning commenced. Mr. Buchanan, the builder, came out from Edgemont one evening with drawings and price estimates. My parents talked late into the evening with him. Mother knew she wanted four bedrooms, electric lights, a bathroom with running water, a fireplace, a built-in buffet-cupboard with a pass-through from the kitchen, a parlor, a dining room, a kitchen with pantry, and a study for Father. Father was aghast and said such ideas were out of the question.

"Why not have what you want? Our children should be brought up in a decent house. I can teach until we get it paid for," Mother said.

By the time Mr. Buchanan left, it had been decided we would have a hollow-tile, square, two-story house with a basement, four bedrooms upstairs and one down, and everything else Mother wanted. A Delco dynamo would be installed in the basement for electric lights. If we could get a good well, we would have running water and a modern bathroom. Against his instinct for making do when it came to our housing, Father signed the contract.

Chapter 33

The Indians

The Fall River County Fair, more a rodeo than a traditional fair, was held every September, and visitors and cowboys came from far and wide. It was the last day, and all the best riders were scheduled to compete.

We sat down in the cool shade of the high roof and watched the quarter-horse races, which were already under way. The calf roping, which we didn't enjoy nearly as much, came next. We admired the smart horses that stood staunchly while each rider tied his calf, but Father cringed visibly each time the young animals were hurled to the ground.

The travois race came next. Five Indian women rode onto the race track astride ponies that had two long poles attached to their sides. They crossed over the ponies' necks and trailed on the ground behind. Blanket rolls or canvas-bound packs lay across the poles behind the horses. The women were seated on bright-colored blankets fastened to the horses by surcingle straps.

They lined up. At the sound of the starting pistol, the ponies, their riders, and the travois went flying around the track. The women whipped their ponies with switches and crowded each other for position on the rail. Dust rolled up

211

behind the poles dragging on the track. The blanket rolls, still firmly fastened to the poles, bounced high. The crowd stood and cheered for the slim young girl with the swinging braids and the oldest rider with the apple-wrinkled face as they raced neck and neck toward the finish line. The old woman won by a hair and accepted her trophy without even a glance at the crowd.

There was a swell of excitement in the stands when the bronco-riding contests began. One by one, the wild horses were released from the chutes with riders on their backs. Some bucked hardly at all and were a disappointment to the rider and crowd, but many were vicious and terrible in their fights to dislodge their riders. Sharp spurs raked their ribs at every leap and made their sides and shoulders bleed, yet they fought on. Some were frothy with sweat from the violence of the battle. Often the rider was tossed off, and the still-bucking bronco, circled the track before being herded back to a corral.

"I've had about enough of this," Father said, coughing in the dusty air.

"The handbill said the Indian women would race after the bucking broncos. Let's stay to see what this is, at least," Mother said. "I don't remember anything like that last year. Then we'll go. Please?"

Before Father could object, four wagons rattled onto the track. These were old-fashioned covered wagons without the canvas stretched over the bows. A woman sat on the high wooden bench of each wagon and drove her team toward the starting line.

A man seated behind us leaned forward and explained, "They use those prairie schooners to haul their tents and to travel to and from the reservations, and sometimes they even live in them for awhile. To have status, a brave must have a horse, but he isn't a man until his squaw has a wagon to drive."

"They certainly haven't seen paint for some time," Father said, "and they rattle as though they are about to fall apart."

They didn't fall apart. The women stood up on the wagons and swung long whips as they whooped and shouted at the horses. The dust almost hid the wagons from sight. They rattled and swung around the race track three times at breakneck speed.

"Oh, those two are going to run into each other," Mother cried. The crowd stood to watch the war going on between two drivers on the far side of the track.

"What happened? What happened?" Verna and I couldn't see anything but people's backs.

"The fat one's winning!" Mother shouted, trying to be heard above the screaming crowd. "She swung in, right in front of the other one. She's ahead, and the other one will never be able to catch up." Sure enough, the oversized Indian woman won the race with her dangerous maneuver.

Everyone sat back down to await the wild-horse races, which were the big-money event of the day. The cowboy had to halter and saddle a horse never saddled before, and with only the halter rope for guidance, be the first to get his horse completely around the track. Kicking, bucking, squealing horses were half dragged or driven out onto the track. Each horse was lassoed to the saddle horn of another rider, and a second rider sandwiched the wild horse between the trained horses.

Sometimes one of the cowboys acted as a hazer. He let his trained horse do the shouldering while he dismounted, grabbed the ears of the wild horse, and "eared him down." This was dangerous. It meant twisting the horse's ears so that he held his head down, tying a bandana over its eyes, and pressing the horse's head against the cowboy's body so the frightened horse could not see.

With the wild horse calmed and steadied by the other horses and temporarily immobilized by the hazers, the bronco rider had to get a halter and saddle on his wild horse and mount it by climbing over the backs of the other horses. Once the lassoes were loosened, the rider and bronco were on their own. The hazers swung their Stetsons, shouted, and did anything they could to get the wild horse started in the right direction.

Ten or fifteen such wild horses and riders were on the track. The broncs bucked and balked in wild-eyed confusion. Some ran, took off, and then ran back into the crowd of riders still trying to saddle up. It was a violent melee of horses and men.

It was dangerous for bystanders too. One horse threw itself through the high wooden fence at the end of the grandstand. It was a miracle that the cowboys standing there were not injured. The rider rolled off the horse as it went down, recovered to his feet, and checked his horse for injuries. As the stunned animal rose, he leapt into the saddle and rejoined the battle.

I was mesmerized by the powerful, wild horses and the skilled, brave cowboys, but Father couldn't stand the violence. He'd had enough, and our day at the fair came to an end.

Chapter 34

The Flu

In the autumn of 1918, the whole country was in the midst of a flu epidemic. The Spanish Flu had already killed hundreds in the army training camps. It hit close to home when Charlie Martin asked Father to hold his soldier brother's funeral. A week after the funeral, Mother received a telegram from Grandpa. *Come at once*, it said. Her mother had the flu.

Within an hour, Mother was packed and ready to catch the No. 43, which Mr. Linaman, the telegraph operator in Provo, had promised to flag down.

We all felt lonesome for her as soon as she left. That evening, as we prepared supper, my admiration for my father teetered a bit when I noticed he didn't know how to crack an egg for frying. I looked on with wonder as he tried to cut it open with a knife. After supper, in the lamplight, he drew pictures for us—sketches of birds, flowers, and scenes of Ireland, including a maid in a cap wheeling a pram. The lovely images returned him to favor in my mind.

The phone rang before we were up the next morning. Mr. Linaman had a message from Mother. Grandma had died during the night. Our hearts were broken. We had loved Grandma dearly. It felt impossible that we would never see her again. Father tried to comfort us, but Verna and I were inconsolable without Mother.

"Mother is suffering more than we are," Father reminded us. "It's her mother who has gone to heaven. We must try to forget how badly we feel and comfort her when she comes home. Grandma was a dear person, but so is your wonderful Mother. We must help her every way we can."

I went to bed early that night with an aching head and ears. When I awoke the next morning, I felt feverish. I put a damp, cold washcloth on my forehead, as I knew Mother would have done, but it didn't help much. By the next morning, I was no better.

"I'd better call Mrs. Stalford," Father said. "I don't feel very well either."

Mrs. Stalford had a gauze pad tied over her nose and mouth when she came into the bedroom to see me. "It's a mask," she said, "to protect me in case you have the flu. It's supposed to screen out some of the germs in the air, but I wonder about that. She touched my forehead and put a thermometer in my mouth. When she looked at my temperature, she went to the door and told Mr. Stalford to go on home without her.

I was very sick for two days, and Father's fever grew worse each day. Mrs. Stalford telephoned Mr. Sykes to send one of the boys over to do our chores. When neighbors called, she warned them away.

As I started to feel better, Verna got sick. On the third day, Father didn't get out of bed at all and couldn't eat. I heard Mrs. Stalford telephone Mr. Linaman and ask him to wire Mother and tell her Father had the flu.

Compared to all of us, who were not very lively, Mother entered the house the next day like a whirlwind. "So glad to be home, even if my family is sick." She hugged each of us in turn.

"You look peaked, Lenna. Should you be up? Verna, how are you? You two little ones are peppy enough. Now let's see about Papa." She hung her coat and hat on the hooks by the door and swept into the bedroom where Father lay shivering from chills under piles of quilts.

As usual, Mother never caught the flu. Roy and Dorothy had a two-day fever and soon were well again. Father recovered slowly. Fortunately, he did not have the pneumonia that killed Grandma and so many others.

The flu killed many people in Edgemont and in the surrounding towns that fall. We had been fortunate, but Father's health did not immediately recover. The fever had damaged the muscles in his left leg, which caused him a lot of pain. He had to use a cane, so Mother and Verna and I helped with chores and outdoor work as much as we could.

One day in early November, Father and I were mending a fence along the road when Myron Howel drove past in his lumber wagon much faster than the bumpy ruts allowed. He stood up, whooped a cowboy yell, and swung his Stetson round and round above his head.

"The war is over! The war is over! Whoopee! The war is over!" he shouted, and rattled on past us toward Provo.

Four weeks later, a veteran named Adolph Pederson came into our lives. He'd taken advantage of the government's offer of homestead land for doughboys and filed a claim nearby. The land wasn't good for farming, but Adolph, with youthful enthusiasm, was doing the things he should to prove up the claim.

In the store one day, Mother overheard him talking about how bored he was, living all alone in his claim shack, and how much he wished he had something to do. Mother suggested he come to our place to help out.

Father soon discovered Adolph didn't know much about farm work, but he was strong and willing to learn. Verna and I were charmed by Adolph's good manners. He was well educated, intelligent, careful about his appearance, and cheerful. He carried a picture of his sweetheart in his wallet—an ethereal blonde young lady living in Yankton, his hometown—and he showed it to Verna and me at every opportunity.

Adolph injected a sense of fun that had gone missing since we lost Bessie. Music had always been a natural part of our lives, but the piano had been silent, and the only singing we did was in church. Verna and I could play the songs in *The South Dakota Community Song Book* on the piano, but the only sheet music we were familiar with was an occasional piano solo Mother ordered from the McKinley Music Company in Chicago. Adolph began to bring copies of popular music to us.

"I'm not sure some of those songs are fit for our girls to play and sing," Father objected.

"Some of them are sort of trashy," Mother said, "but I don't think the words are that bad. They're just silly, and some of the melodies are beautiful. The girls should know this sort of music too. Don't worry about it. It's part of being young."

Verna and I were thrilled with the music Adolph introduced us to. We had only heard our parents' songs. They sometimes sang duets at special church programs. Father could play the piano by ear and read tenor parts or bass by note position. He had brought his violin from Ireland and could fiddle "Irish Washer Woman" or "The Wearin' O' the Green" as well as most fiddlers. He was shy about this, however, and played only for us. Occasionally, when he was in the mood, he'd favor us with an Irish jig, the high point of which was him kicking off one of his carpet slippers and deftly catching it again on a toe.

Mother was accomplished on the piano and organ. She had a strong alto voice, but could read and sing any part. She knew lots of songs by heart, and if there was no piano or organ, she was always the one to start the tune. She taught us children to play the piano and know the notes as soon as we could read words, and we were often asked to sing or play duets in public.

Adolph brought all that wonderful music back into our house. He was impatient sometimes with our inability to "jazz it up," but we improved, and, more and more when the Cass family or others came to spend the evening, we gathered around the piano and sang popular music with the other children. At milking time, anyone going by our corral could have heard three-part renditions of "Long, Long Trail," "O Let the Rest of the World Go By," "Smiles," and "Home on the Range" accompanied by rhythmic streams of milk hitting the pails.

Chapter 35

The Fall of 1919

Mother and I were driving home from school in the buggy one warm fall day when she tightened her grip on the reins and sat straight up. A man was approaching on horseback, kicking his piebald, urging it on.

"Must be a Cavinder sheepherder," she said under her breath.

The man met us halfway up the last hill before our homestead. His black, wide-brimmed hat dipped low over a rough, unshaven face. He rode hunched over and pulled up his heavy-footed horse at the side of our buggy.

"Ma'am." He tipped his hat. "Do you know anything about Jim Roberts? I tend sheep near his place, and I buy eggs and milk from him, but today, I can't find him anywhere."

Mother nodded. "Sure, we know Jim and Minnie. But we haven't seen him for awhile. He kind of keeps to himself."

"Yes, ma'am," he said with some impatience. "Something must have happened to him. The house door and windows are open, and his team is half starved, tied in the barn."

Mother looked up the draw toward the tar-papered Roberts buildings and shook her head. "I can't imagine."

"I looked around at Jim's pretty good. Everything's a mess. Rained in during that last storm, I guess, and things are blown around."

"We live right over the hill here. I'll call around and see what I can find out." Mother slapped her horse with the reins. "We'll get somebody up there right away. Thanks for telling us."

"I got to get back to my sheep. Sure hope Jim is all right," he said and trotted away.

Mother telephoned the nearest neighbors, and when Father came home, he joined in the search. It wasn't long before he returned.

"Dearie, put out a general alarm on the telephone. Jim has disappeared. Must have been gone a long time. His starved team ate holes right through the wooden mangers. One is dying right there by the water hole—too weak to drink. We've got to get a search party organized. Call the sheriff. I'm going back. We must do all we can before dark."

He turned his horse and was off again as he shouted, "See if you can find out anything from Minnie."

After we finished the chores, Verna and I played Ant'ny Over, throwing the ball over the roof of the house with little interest. We kept looking at the Robert's house in the distance, mysterious and black against the darkening horizon. Now and then we caught sight of dim figures walking and riding through the Roberts's fields and pastures.

The cool night wind had driven us into the shelter of the house when Father finally came riding home. His shoulders drooped as he got off Doc's back. In the light of Mother's lamp, deep shadows gouged his cheeks.

"We found him up there on the hill, in the corner of his pasture. His milk pail and stool lay beside him. Evidently he'd gone up there to milk his cow. Maybe lightning struck him during that last storm. Maybe he had a heart attack. We left him there. The sheriff is calling for the undertaker."

"Lenna, unsaddle Doc, and turn him out for your Father. Verna, you help. Here's the lantern." She linked her arm in Father's. "I have supper waiting for you, Joe. The chores are all done."

Verna and I raced to unsaddle Doc. We didn't want to miss a thing. The Sunday before, we had disobeyed Mother and gone farther from home than we had promised. We'd picked flowers directly across from where poor old Mr. Roberts lay dead in the grass. I shivered at the thought that we could have been the ones to find him.

"Still haven't located Minnie," Mother was saying as we hurried into the house.

"Poor woman. She'll be lost without Jim. He was her whole life," Father said. "Jim must have died suddenly, but those poor animals—even the chickens, with free run of the place, are half starved. The cow is all right, though near dry with a caked udder. But those horses—I'll never forget the sight of the poor things. The sheriff thinks Jim died at least ten days ago. The milk pail had been battered by hail, so it was likely out there during that last big storm."

The next afternoon the sheriff brought Minnie Roberts to our house. She wanted to know what the sheepherder had said to Mother. Her wig was askew and her face was red and puffy.

"It wasn't an accident," she said, mopping her wet eyes. "Somebody killed him. I know it."

Verna and I stood and squirmed. I'd never seen anybody so upset.

Sobs overcame her again, and Mother patted her shoulder. "I shouldn't have left him alone. It's my fault."

Minnie blew her nose in her lace handkerchief. "He wouldn't have gone out into the pasture to milk the cow."

She tucked her hanky in her waistband. "Somebody killed him."

"Now, Minnie, don't say things you'll be sorry for. Just trust and pray. Everyone wants to help you. You're not alone, and don't blame yourself for what has happened," Mother said in her most soothing voice.

Minnie wept and accused by turns—the Cavinder men, the sheepherders, the people Jim had worked for, the neighbors. "He probably was poisoned and was so sick he walked toward your place for help."

That was it. Mother had had enough.

"Now look here, Minnie, if you're accusing the neighbors of poisoning Jim, you really are out of your mind. Can you think of any reason in the world why people would have done such a thing? Can you imagine Mr. O'Neill or anyone leaving animals to suffer the way those horses must have? It's time you got hold of yourself and helped instead of hindering the good people who are trying to help you through this tragedy." Mother added in her most teacherly tone, "I won't listen to anymore of it, Minnie."

Minnie collected herself and drove away with the sheriff after arranging for Father to hold the funeral in Edgemont on Monday.

Before the month was up, Father received a letter from Minnie accusing him of poisoning Jim in an attempt to take over his land. "I'm having Jim's body disinterred and an analysis made in Omaha to see if he was poisoned," she wrote. "Be prepared to be called into court."

"The woman's insane," Father cried. "The idea!"

Word got around, and for the next few weeks the neighbors laughed and teased Father about his wickedness. Father fumed!

Minnie did have Jim's body exhumed. No trace of poison was found, but Minnie had poisoned all her relationships in the valley. None of us ever wanted to see her again.

Chapter 36

The Accident

I n early August, Father and Adolph began cutting grain at the Gladson place. The Gladson brothers had moved back to Iowa, and Father purchased 320 acres of their best land. With 1100 acres, Father had far more work than he could handle by himself, so Adolph became our full-time hired man.

I drove the Model T down to the field in the afternoon, bringing a jug of lemonade to the men working in the hot, blistering wind. Adolph had been teaching Verna and me to drive so we could run errands across the far-flung fields for Father. I parked and waited for the binder to come to the end of the field.

The reel of the binder rotated steadily through the rippling grain, and in the strong west wind, dust rose and blew ahead of the men and the machine. A powdery coating whitened the black car cushion beside me. Father had nearly reached the end of the row when I became aware of another cloud of dust approaching across the fresh-cut stubble. Mr. Howell was riding his white mule toward us as fast as the creature could go. He rode right up to the tractor, shouting and gesturing. Father jumped off the tractor and ran down the field toward me.

"The baby's poisoned!" he cried. "Swallowed carbolic acid."

He jerked the car door open, started the motor, and drove recklessly across the stubble toward Howell's. "Mr. Howell left his gates open for us," he shouted. We swayed and bounced across the field. The dust choked me. I crawled onto the back seat and threw myself face down, terrified.

"Pray, Lenna! We must pray!"

The car went so fast the seat cushion bounced loose. The tools in the tool box below me banged into each other, making a terrible noise. I rolled off the cushion and lay on the floor boards, sobbing, gasping, and trying to pray. "Please God, help my little sister. Dear God, help us!"

I kept my head covered, crouched on the floor. We must have passed through Howell's last gate and reached the road, because the way got smoother. The bouncing wasn't so bad now, but Father drove faster. The car tipped wildly as we swerved around a corner. I guessed we were at Old Man Jahns' place. Then Father screeched to a halt.

I unwound myself and looked out. Cars, wagons, and buggies had jammed into our yard. The men of our neighborhood leaned against their vehicles, arms folded, talking. Father dashed into the house. I climbed into the front seat, turned off the motor, and scrambled out of the car.

I found Mother and Father in the lean-to. "We're waiting for the doctor," Mother said. She didn't even look like herself. Her eyes shone like the headlights on the Model T, and her skin glistened with sweat. "The Disbrows sent word up to the schoolhouse, and everybody came over from the town meeting at Provo." She was talking really fast, like I'd never heard her.

Father looked past her. "Where's Dorothy? Where's the baby?"

She turned to him in slow motion, as if she was moving through water, as if his words took a moment to reach her ears.

"Verna has her. She doesn't seem to be in pain. Her lips are all blistered."

Father wheeled around. "But where is she?" he shouted, his voice filled with fear.

"I've got her, Reverend O'Neill." Mrs. Disbrow appeared from the parlor. "She seems to like the coolness of this starched dress of mine."

Dorothy smiled wanly at Father, and then leaned against the starched bosom again. She looked gray and exhausted, but she didn't cry.

"I called the doctor right away," Mother said.

"Now, Dearie," Father said, putting his arm around her.

Mother couldn't stop talking, though her voice trembled, and the words came out in halting rushes. "I had Roy and her playing in a tub of water on the cistern platform. It's such a hot day! I went back into the house to finish my sewing, and Verna was there with me, reading a book. Suddenly, Dorothy screamed, and when I ran out, I saw Roy standing there with the empty blue carbolic acid bottle. He said he'd poured the medicine into the water, so I snatched her out, but then her lips began to blister, and she screamed and screamed, and I realized she might have swallowed some of it."

My heart beat so loud it echoed in my ears. Mrs. Disbrow wouldn't give Dorothy to me and shushed me when I tried to speak. I never felt so scared and helpless.

Mother kept right on. "How could Roy have climbed up to the cupboard without my seeing him? He had a stool on top of the high chair! Oh, Joe!"

Now Father saw that her right arm and hand were wrapped with a cloth bandage. "My goodness, Dearie! What—"

"She has a terrible burn," Mrs. Disbrow said. "I sure wish that doctor would get here."

"The doctor told me to make her drink cream or warm lard," Mother said. "I put the lard on the stove to warm, while I tried to get her to drink the cream. She just cried and cried and wouldn't take it. I finally got some down her, and she threw up. Then the lard caught fire, and when I snatched the cup, the hot lard spilled down my arm."

Father looked like he was about to cry he was so upset and worried about Mother and Dorothy.

"Don't worry about me," she said to Father. Then, she noticed me for the first time since I walked in. "Lenna, will you see if you can find Roy? He's outside somewhere."

I found Roy forlorn, sobbing, and hiding behind the side door. I carried him inside the screened porch and sat down on the cot, holding him close, rocking him, comforting him, and crying with him. I thought my heart would burst with fear for my sister. I believed she might die in Mrs. Disbrow's arms, and I couldn't bear it. And Mama—I saw the pain in her eyes and knew her arm must hurt terribly. "Dear little Roy, don't cry. You didn't mean to do wrong. We love you. Don't cry."

I looked up and saw the doctor's car drive into the yard. "He's here! The doctor's here," I called out. I raced back to the lean-to with Roy still in my arms. The doctor grabbed his black bag and ran in ahead of me.

"No need to worry," I heard him say. "This little girl is going to be just fine." It had taken him no more than a second to look inside her mouth and see that there were no burns. "She couldn't have swallowed any of the acid. Those lip burns will heal in a hurry." He turned to Mother. "Now, Mrs. O'Neill, let's have a look at that arm. I think you're the one who needs medical attention."

One by one, the cars and buggies and wagons drove out of the yard.

"How wonderful to have such good friends," said Father. He was exuberant, released from the terror that had gripped all of us. "They would have helped any way they could."

He turned to Mother. "Now what can I do to help you, Dearie?" She waved him off, smiling.

"Well, Roy, what have you been crying about? Never saw such a tear-stained face. Come here, my boy." Father lifted him up and kissed him.

"My word," Father exclaimed. "Here comes Adolph."

Father and I had forgotten him at the Gladson place, and he'd had to walk all the way.

Adolph and Father embraced, which was just one more thing I'd never seen. "You forgot more than me," Adolph said, chuckling. "Mr. O'Neill, you even forgot to turn off the tractor. But who cares, so long as the baby is all right."

We all agreed with Adolph. As long as we had each other, the hot weather, the hard work, the debts, the problems of the new house, and even physical pain—none of it mattered, and all of it could be endured.

Chapter 37

Sarah

Adolph looked pale and tired. He'd spent the night at the hotel in Edgemont and brought out more men to work on the construction of our new house.

"I really had a night last night," he said, as he downed the glass of milk Mother poured him. "A young girl had a baby in the hotel room next to mine. I didn't know having a baby was that awful. That girl screamed and cried."

Mother glanced over at us and tried to shoo us away with a quick shake of her head, but we didn't budge. "Poor dear," she said.

Verna and I were all ears.

"There was coming and going all night," he said. "I didn't sleep at all. This morning at the desk, the man told me she had been on the train going east when she realized her time had come. She'd gotten off at Edgemont and taken the hotel room. She tried to have that baby all by herself, Mrs. O'Neill, but the hotel folks heard—how could they help it?—and sent for the doctor."

"Well, thank goodness they did," Mother said.

"I think there's something wrong. She didn't stop crying all night. It's none of my business, but I'm sure sorry for that girl."

Mother called the doctor and the hotel, put on her good dress, and drove the Model T back to town.

A few days later, Sarah and her fatherless baby came to live with us.

"She has no place else to go, at least until the baby is adopted. She won't bring shame on her family back in Montana. They think she's a waitress in Alliance," Mother explained to Father.

"It's all right, but I hope she really helps you and is not just a burden," Father said.

Sarah was a shy, withdrawn girl, but she was good help and took excellent care of her baby. The house construction brought on a lot of extra housework. Some of the men brought lunches and went home each night, but others were drifters, willing to do the labor for lower wages if food and a bed were furnished. One or two were always with us for meals.

In the midst of all this activity on the homestead, we got a surprise visit. The threshing was in full swing, and Mother had just tidied up after feeding the crew their dinner when Uncle Carl drove his shiny new touring car into our yard. He and Aunt Beth and her brother Chris and his wife had driven from Laurel, Nebraska, for an impromptu visit.

"Hello, Dora," Uncle Carl shouted jovially through the screen door.

Mother gasped. "Well, of all things." Uncle Carl gave her a kiss on the cheek with a big smack, and then called to the others in the car, "Come on in."

"Yes, do come in," Mother cried joyfully.

The excitement woke the baby, who was napping on the porch with Sarah.

"A baby," Aunt Beth exclaimed, her eyes wide with surprise.

Mother explained in a hushed voice as she poured lemonade left over from the threshers' dinner. In a few minutes, she called Sarah in. The baby in her arms looked even more beautiful than usual, and the ladies from Nebraska oohed and aahed and immediately fell in love.

"I knew Beth would be happy once we got here. Now she's baby happy besides," Uncle Carl said, laughing. "Guess you've got overnight guests, Dora. We men better go help with the threshing. We're darned good supervisors, if nothing else, eh, Chris?"

The supper table was lively with talk and laughter, but it had been a long trip for the Nebraska people and a hard day for Mother and Father.

"Well, Dora, I hope you have an extra quilt or two," Uncle Carl said. "I know where I'm going to sleep tonight—out in that beautiful strawstack. Best mattress in the world. Been waiting for a chance to do that ever since I was a little boy."

"You're not going out there without me," Aunt Beth said with great enthusiasm.

Chris and his wife said they wanted to stay out there too.

Father protested he couldn't let company sleep in a strawstack, but everyone else thought it was a lark. Besides, there wasn't anywhere else for them to stay. Mother loaded Chris and his wife with bedding and gave them a flashlight, and they went out into the star-filled night to make their bed on the fresh straw still fragrant with the sweet aroma of newly harvested wheat.

Uncle Carl and Aunt Beth lingered awhile and talked in low voices with Mother and Father. In bed in the lean-to,

I listened to their laughter and joking. Smothered laughter drifted back to the house after they said their good nights and fixed their beds in the straw. After a while, the cool light of the rising moon set a few coyotes to yapping, and I heard no more from the outdoor pajama party.

Our visitors left right after breakfast. Aunt Beth's father had land in Wyoming that she'd never seen. They promised to stop again on their way back.

That afternoon, I found Sarah packing her things.

"Where are you going?" I asked, amazed.

"I'm going to Alliance. That letter that came last week told me of a waitress job there. Now the baby is strong—" her voice broke, "—and your wonderful mother has promised to care for it awhile."

"No," I exclaimed, not daring to believe I'd heard right.

"I'll come back and see you all someday," she said in a hoarse whisper, turning her tear-stained face away from me.

I waved goodbye to her as she rode away in the Model T with Father to catch the train in Provo, and I never saw her again.

The next day, the Nebraska folks came back.

"We must go right on if we're going to get that baby home by tomorrow noon," Uncle Carl said. He handed Mother an envelope. "Please mail this to your Sarah."

I ran to the barn, threw an arm around Duke's neck, and wept into his mane. Mother called for me, and I wiped my tears as best I could before going out to say good-bye to the relatives. Aunt Beth looked down at the baby in her arms with unrestrained joy, and I knew I must be glad for Sarah and her child.

Chapter 38

Women's Rights

Dora O'Neill

M other was asked to serve as an election clerk for the first national election since the ratification of the Nineteenth Amendment. South Dakota women had been granted their voting rights in 1918, but this was their first opportunity to cast ballots for a new president. Mother had been an outspoken supporter of women's rights. Some of the men looked askance at her boldness and probably made unkind remarks about Dearie O'Neill, but everyone respected her intelligence and common sense. Without a doubt, she was the best educated woman in the valley.

She was preparing to set out on horseback on a bitter, November morning. Sleet and snow covered the already-deep snow on the ground. The car couldn't get through the drifts on the roads. The buggy could have cut through, but if it continued to snow all day, the trip home would be impossible.

"Well, if I have to, I have to," said Mother, struggling into her Montgomery Ward coveralls. Verna and I had never seen Mother ride a horse, and we couldn't believe she was willing to be seen in those coveralls. She tucked her voluminous dress inside and pulled on a sweater. Father held her coat, and she slipped into it with some difficulty. All those layers created so much bulk she had to use one of Father's belts instead of buttoning it. She pulled the wool cap over her hair and wrapped the muffler around her neck.

After giving each of us our instructions for the day— schoolwork, chores, supper—she kissed us all and went out the door. "Haven't been on a horse since I was a girl. Don't you experts laugh now," she called out as she climbed onto Doc and headed over to the polling place at the Plains Valley School.

We children squinted through the snow and sleet rattling against the dining room window to see if we could see Mother riding astride a horse, but in the early morning darkness and through the gray storm, we could barely make out the blurred outline of Mother and Doc going out the yard gate. We turned to our oatmeal grown cold.

Father came in from chores with tiny icicles hanging from his mustache. "That mother of yours! She's a wonder! Who else in all the world would think it an adventure to ride a horse in this sort of weather just to spend all day with three men watching people vote. She's going to be stiff too after riding that far. She'll make a joke of it, but she'll be sore all right."

He warmed his hands at the stove as he talked, and he turned almost fiercely toward Verna and me washing the breakfast dishes. "Girls, don't you ever find anything in your hearts but pride for your mother. She's the bravest, smartest, most wonderful woman you'll ever know." I knew his stern gaze reflected his deep love for Mother, not disapproval of us.

I waited until Father went back outside before I dared bring up Mother's wardrobe. "How do you suppose Mother will get those Montgomery Ward coveralls off once she gets there? She'll never take them off in front of those men."

"Hadn't thought of that," said Verna. "Gentlemen, kindly turn your backs while I remove my Montgomery Ward coveralls," she joked. "Or maybe she'll say, 'Fellow voters, my pants are too tight. Kindly lower your eyes while I remove them.'"

"Shame on you." I stifled a laugh as I pictured Mother peeling off her pants before an audience.

"She'll figure something out," Verna said. "Like she says, 'Necessity is the mother of invention.'" Verna repeated Mother's favorite saying in her most deeply dramatic tones and floated the dish towel like a banner from her outstretched arm. She was definitely becoming the actress of the family.

As the morning went on, the sleet no longer shattered against the windows. Instead, great gobs of wet snow dropped off the eaves. At noon, the snow turned to cold rain, then the wind and intermittent rain ended, and the temperature began to drop. Gray snow clouds moved eastward in the frozen skies, and a weak sun hung in a clean cold strip of blue-gold at the horizon. Father hurried with the evening chores, saddled Duke, and took off to vote and bring Mother home.

"Such an interesting day," said Mother cheerfully, as she peeled off her extra layers of clothing and her face turned pink again in the warmth of the house. "Wouldn't have missed it for the world. Everybody in the township voted. I'll bet that's a record. I think the men didn't want to be outdone by the women."

"Oh, you women," Father teased, parroting "Oh, you kid," the slang phrase making the rounds.

"I surely got sick of tobacco smoke. What a horrible habit." Mother chattered on.

"Better sit down and eat," I interrupted. "Everything has been warming for so long it's pretty dried out."

Mother had so much to tell, she went right on. "We counted all the ballots before we left—Papa wasn't too happy about having to wait—and if the whole county votes the way our township did, Warren G. Harding will be the next President."

We plied Mother with questions as we ate our supper, and she relived her day for us. Her voice and face reflected the joy we often observed when she had a new and stimulating experience.

"Well, lady politician, you haven't mentioned the pleasures of riding Doc as an accomplishment of the day," Father said.

Mother scoffed and laughed.

"You're more tired than you think. We'd better get to bed. Come on, girls. Ask the rest of your questions tomorrow," Father said.

"Just one more," Verna pleaded. "With those men around, how did you take off the Montgomery Ward coveralls?"

She snapped her fingers. "Easy. I went behind a curtain in the vestibule where the children hang their coats. It made an excellent dressing room. Necessity is the mother of invention, you know."

Chapter 39

The Christmas Corset

Father and I balanced the big wooden box as it slid from the tailgate of the lumber wagon down the slanting plank. Verna held the door open, and we shoved the gigantic box into the house.

"My goodness, what a big box this time," Mother said.

Although Father had resigned his pastorate in Edgemont long ago, we continued to receive the missionary boxes. One arrived in the spring and the other between Thanksgiving and Christmas. This year there had been no box in the spring, and we had wondered if the boxes were at an end. Mother had written to the Home Mission Society telling them they should send their donations to preacher's families, and yet, here was the biggest missionary box we'd ever received.

"We'll have to open it right here in the lean-to," said Father as he took off his coat and mittens. "It's just too heavy to move farther." He rubbed the cold from his hands, took up his crowbar, and attacked the box. Nails screeched and wood shuttered as he pried up board after board, pulled out the nails, and laid the wood aside. He saved every bit of wood and each nail for use another day.

"Lenna, it's your turn to take the first thing out," Mother said. Somehow she remembered from year to year. I folded back the heavy paper, trying hard to be slow and careful, but wanting to rip into it in my excitement. A pink-striped chiffon blouse trimmed with black beads lay on top, and it called to me.

Verna drew in her breath. "Oh, pretty! Will it fit you, Mama?"

"Oh, dear. Too small, I think," said Mother holding it up to herself. "We'll let Lenna have it."

Everyone got a turn dipping into the box, and each item was inspected and admired or disdained, then set aside to be used at once, grown into, or altered and worn later. Mother marveled at elaborate silk dresses, some with Paris labels, and long white kid gloves to go with them. She found a soft blue-beaver felt hat that she planned to wear to the Christmas program that very night and a murky blackish-brown velour coat as soft as fur.

We found dresses for Verna and me and outfits for the baby and Roy. There was a suit that Mother was sure she could alter in the seat and shoulders to fit Father plus several stiff white shirts with removable collars and cuffs.

To my delight, there were several boned lace corsets. They were not at all the utilitarian sort of thing Mother wore. One was especially exquisite. Its stiff-boned waist curved gracefully. Dangling garters hung below the ruffles and scalloped embroidery trimmed the top. It was shell pink with long side and back laces. This was the most feminine-looking garment I had ever seen. I held it up to see if it could possibly be my size. It obviously wasn't meant for Mother's more ample proportions. Mother glanced at me and laughed, "You'll have to do some growing before that will fit you, child."

In addition to the corsets, the box included items from a life so far removed from our own we couldn't imagine using them. For instance, a small pasteboard box contained a long gray feather boa coiled like a snake. A leather case held mother-of-pearl opera glasses. Two bisque statuettes, a shepherd boy and a maiden with a basket, were wrapped in paper and tucked into the folds of a pair of lace curtains. Knowing we'd never have an occasion to wear them, Verna and I nevertheless admired several pairs of high-heeled pointed-toed shoes that looked like they'd never touched the ground.

In addition to the cast-off items, the box included store-bought underwear for all the family along with woolen nightshirts and nightgowns, stockings, socks, handkerchiefs, and a box of chocolate turkeys that made us squeal with glee. We thought we'd unpacked everything. Then Father noticed the brown paper that lined the bottom was wrapped around something. He removed the paper and pulled out a plush, dark-green auto robe.

"How wonderful," Father said. "Wait. Here's a note pinned to it: *For the Ford automobile. Harriet G. Magna, Holyoke, Massachusetts.*"

"Aunt Harriet!" We shouted in unison. She had mailed us the down payment for the Model T, and once again, had sent us a special gift. Verna and I felt sure she had sent us the chocolate turkeys too.

Father reminded us that we still had chores to do before early supper and the Christmas program in Provo. The lovely corset was put away with the beaded blouse and the Paris gowns to wait for the day when they would be put to use.

I bundled up against the cold and went out to the barn. It felt good to lean close to Brindle's warm body. Steam rose as the warm milk hit the cold pail. I hurried through the milking, hung up the stool, and hastened to the house. Father had finished too and was not far behind me, carrying his pail of milk and the lantern.

"Supper's ready. If we don't dawdle, we'll be in plenty of time," called Mother. I looked forward to seeing all my friends at the schoolhouse for the community Christmas program— church, school, and literary society combined. Verna and I were going to sing a duet.

I rushed through supper. "I'll get dressed first and help wipe the dishes afterwards, if it's all right," I said.

"Good idea. Then we won't be in each other's way," Mother said.

I excused myself and closed the door to the bedroom. Before entering the part curtained off for Verna and me, I stopped at Mother's dresser and slipped the pink corset out of the pile of garments from the box.

I wasn't sure whether it should go over my head or be pulled up over my hips. Either way, it didn't present any obstacles from either direction. I slithered into it head first. As I'd expected, the corset wasn't a tight fit no matter how hard I pulled on the laces. I did admire how it created curves where I had none. Regardless of the loose fit, I tied the laces into neat bows and fastened the garters to my black lisle stockings. The corset made them look quite glamorous, I thought, but the garters were too long. For safety's sake, I pulled on my round elastic garters too. After one last look at my grown-up self in the mirror, I threw on my petticoat, my waist-topped skirt, and my blouse and slipped back into the main room to help with dishes. Discomfort aside, I felt extremely stylish and tossed aside any doubts about the wisdom of my plan.

On the way to the program, Verna and I pulled the new auto robe around us against the chill from the side curtains.

The cold didn't bother me much, but the longer I sat, the higher the corset rose. Before long, I felt as though my arms were hanging over the edge of a barrel.

When I stood up to get out of the car at the schoolhouse, the corset slipped back where it had been, but now, with every step I took, it crept lower. Squeezing my elbows tight against my body, I slipped into a school desk beside Verna. The corset shot up under my arms again.

"I'm glad we're early on the program," Verna whispered. "It's too hot in here."

I was glad to know that I wasn't the only one who was hot and uncomfortable.

After the opening prayer and Scriptures, Father, much to my relief, announced that since the room was so crowded, we would remain seated while we sang "O Little Town of Bethlehem."

Two boys presented a dialogue about hanging up their stockings for Christmas, and then it was time for our duet. I had lost all confidence that the pink monstrosity would stay in place, for it seemed to have developed a mind of its own. I sat down at the organ and began pumping the foot pedals, when I realized the corset had shifted. I imagined everyone in the room staring at that bulge on my bosom, misplaced and slightly to one side. I hunched forward in an effort to conceal it. "Oh, star of the East," I wailed, struggling to stay in tune as the stays stabbed me. The anguish in my voice didn't disturb Verna. She just sang louder, and I let her alto overtake my soprano for a resounding finish.

I clutched my sides with my elbows and followed Verna back to our seat. Eric Cass smiled and nodded at me, but not even romance moved my mind from the instrument of torture that encased me.

At last, the recitations and the pantomime cradle scene ended. The little children marched off the platform carrying the red oilcloth letters that spelled "Merry Christmas." Mr. Coleman, dressed up in Father's Santa Claus suit, burst through the door, accompanied by the din of ringing sleigh bells. He lumbered through the crowd, jingling the bells and greeting the children.

"Who will be Santa's helpers?" The dreaded words stabbed me like the stays of the corset. "How about the O'Neill girls?"

I avoided his eyes, but Verna took an armload of the red stockings and handed half to me. I was trapped. Every time I held out my arms to distribute the goodies, the corset sank lower. I clamped my elbows to my sides and carried on. Somehow I managed, even when I had to lean over to reach an outstretched hand. However, there came a point when I realized that any further exertion would bring catastrophe. If I bent over once more, I would lose the corset altogether. Like a pump handle, my arms moved up and down from my elbows as I distributed the last of the stockings. With tremendous relief, I backed up to a wall and leaned firmly against it.

It seemed an eternity before I heard Father quiet the crowd and say the benediction. I hobbled to the desk, pulled on my coat, clutched my own red-mesh sock full of Christmas candy, and prayed that the corset would stay on as I shuffled through the crowd.

On the ride home, Mother and Father and Verna talked gaily about the evening, while Roy and Dorothy babbled about big Santa and all the candy. I, on the other hand, sat stiff and miserable and silent.

"I was really proud of my girls tonight," Mother said. "But I thought you looked pale, Lenna. Do you feel all right? You've hardly said a word. By the way, there's something wrong with that red blouse. It bunches up in the front. Better remind me to look at it tomorrow."

I pulled the auto robe higher to smother sobs that welled up without warning. I couldn't tell her that a beautiful corset, which was now almost backward and down to my knees, jabbed me with every jolt over the frozen ruts.

That night, I learned the meaning of "There's a place for everything . . ." and that the place for a pink ruffled corset was not on me.

Chapter 40

The New House

The holidays brought us a long-awaited gift. We moved into our new house after the New Year. Father took charge of bringing our furniture over, including the many pieces stored in the shed. Verna and I helped Mother carry everything else, one armload at a time. Each time we opened the door of the new house, we were greeted by the hum of the Delco dynamo in the basement that powered the electric lights. Verna and I got a kick out of pushing the buttons to turn them off and on. The luxury of electricity in our home made us feel proud. We might have taken pride in our indoor plumbing too, but without a well, we had no use for the pristine white porcelain fixtures.

Despite that temporary omission, Mother was in a fever of excitement as the house took shape and became our new home. The kitchen was the best place of all. The malleable steel range Mother had purchased dominated the room. It was Mother's great joy. There were warming ovens above, where she stored her flat irons, stove blacking, and the turkey wing for brushing off the hot cooking surface. A deep reservoir at one side filled with soft rain or snow water provided warm water for dishwashing or baths. The coal fire was never allowed to go out, and in the winter, it kept the shiny teakettle singing all day long. We used the hot water for tea—and to thaw out cars, tractors, and cold hands. When we came in from chores with freezing-cold feet, we opened the oven door and propped them up to catch the warmth. Needless to say, the kitchen was the heart of the house, though we loved every corner of our new home.

Our voices no longer echoed in the empty parlor. The music cabinet with its oval mirror stood beside the piano, across the room from the organ. Mother's bookcase, with the black and gold set of E. P. Roe novels and the red leather-bound classics, occupied the center of one wall. Aunt Lucy's hand-painted vases sat on top, and her charcoal drawing of kittens playing with books hung between them.

For Verna and me, the most exciting thing about the new house was the stairway that led up from the front hall. The polished banister shone in the light from the oval glass window of the front door, and gleaming steps mounted to the second floor. Verna and I knew we were too big to slide down the slippery railing but tried it anyway. We decided that the stories we had read about banister sliding overrated its joys.

"At last, we have room for a party when we want to have one," Mother said. "How about a birthday celebration, Lenna?"

"Oh, can we, Mama?" I pictured my friends gliding down the banister, sitting on the rockers in the parlor, lazing on the velvety-soft flowered rug. However, in the days that followed, nothing more was said about the party, and though I asked about it several times, Mother was always too busy to answer.

School started again, and Verna and I resumed going in turns. On my birthday, Mother took the Model T instead of the

buggy, saying she had something to do after school and wanted
to get home faster than old Don usually brought us. I was glad,
because Mother had made me a coral velvet tam with white
rabbit fur around the head band, and I longed to wear it to
school, but wouldn't have risked it in the open buggy.

At the end of the school day, I was sitting in the car waiting
for Mother, when seemingly out of nowhere, the entire eighth
grade streamed out from behind the schoolhouse and climbed
into our car.

"Surprise! Surprise! We're going to your birthday party!"

At home, Verna had outdone herself preparing for the
guests. The house shone, and she'd dressed Roy and Dorothy
in their best clothes. While Mother and Verna prepared the
birthday supper, I showed my friends around the new house.
We kept repeating the tours so we could end them at the top of
the stairs, and the boys could slide down the banister. The girls
looked as though they'd like to try it too, but being on their
best behavior, they didn't. It was entertaining enough to make
taunting and sarcastic remarks as the boys flew past.

Verna and Father had put all the extra leaves in the dining
room table. The good dishes that had been packed away so
long we didn't recognize them were set on the beautiful lace
tablecloth. The silver was polished to a high shine like the oak
floors, the mantel, even the windows. To me, it looked like the
palace of a princess.

I presided regally from my place at the head of the table.
When Mother brought in the cake lit with thirteen candles, my
heart nearly burst with happiness. One by one, the children
placed their gifts in front of me. Ivan gave me a wooden jewelry
box he'd crafted with the help of his father. Wilbur brought
candy he had made in his mother's kitchen. Marcie had sewed
a ribbon-trimmed apron, and Dottie had crocheted around

the edges of a handkerchief for me. The last gift was from Eric. He'd fashioned a bookmark from a piece of silk and painted flowers and hearts on it along with a printed two-line verse in ink. He had written so small, it was hard to read: "Dear Lenna, I thought of a lovely plan. I'm going to marry you when I'm a man." I blushed deep red, but the fact that he had worked so hard to make this for me choked me with happiness. I didn't dare look at him. "Thank you," I said in a shy whisper. It was all I could squeeze out.

After supper, we played games and sang songs at the piano, just as I had imagined. By the time we all helped clean up the dishes, it was late. Mother reminded us of school the next day.

"You boys will sleep in the hired man's room," Mother said. "Three of you can manage to fit in one bed, can't you? Dottie will sleep with Lenna and Marcie with Verna." In her sternest schoolteacher tone, Mother said, "Now, if there are going to be any pillow fights, they'd better happen before, not after, you're ready for bed."

Pillow fights! We tore up the stairs, swept the pillows from the beds, and attacked each other with a vengeance. A great thumping, throwing, and snatching of Mother's feather-filled pillows commenced. Doors slammed. Girls giggled and squealed. We pelted each other, hid in closets, rolled under beds, and raced from one room to another, breathless and elated.

"All right, you wild ones! Now it's time for bed," Father said. "But before you say your prayers and crawl into bed, there is something I neglected to do." Father marched up the stairs toward me. "It wouldn't be a proper birthday without a spanking, would it?"

I turned to escape—too late. He caught me in his arms and I squirmed and whirled and twisted, but Father overpowered me. The boys gathered around, close enough to catch me if I broke loose. Like a bronc at the rodeo or a calf at branding time, I surrendered.

". . . and one to grow on, and one to be good on!" Father gave me thirteen whacks plus one. "Now, you've had your comeuppance for another year."

I thought for sure the boys would follow suit, and I backed away, trembling.

"Now to bed. All of you," Father said. "She's had her spanking. Say your prayers and go to sleep. We all need rest for tomorrow." Father was a bit breathless from our struggle as he gave me a kiss. "Happy Birthday, good daughter."

Chapter 41

A Quest for Water

Fred Cass and Father were leaning up against the corral fence talking. "You really should have a dam somewhere to insure good water for your stock," Mr. Cass said. "Why don't you put a dam down there in that draw? The boys and I would help you. By next spring you'd, have quite a water supply."

"I've been thinking about putting in a dam, but I thought I should try a well first. Just as soon as I have time, I'll get at it."

There was no rush. The water holes were brim full. With the big snow in April and good rains all spring, there was plenty of moisture in the ground. "Crops will be good again," people assured each other.

Father bought Jim Roberts's range land north of our house, and that spring, three years from the time we had taken claim to it, we proved up on our first homestead land. We could have waited another two years, but Father wanted the land to be legally ours as soon as possible.

We had acquired more cattle and were milking sixteen cows. They were range cows and didn't give a great amount of milk, but Mother skimmed the milk and sold the cream, and the regular cream check helped buy our groceries.

Sugar was beginning to be hard to get. Flour sold for five dollars a bag. Mother used recipes for sugarless desserts and cookies and ground wheat in the coffee grinder to extend the flour for bread making. We had plenty of eggs and jackrabbit meat and vegetables from the garden. We girls helped Mother gather wild plums and chokecherries, and she made choke-cherry jelly, plum butter and sauce, and juice, which she put in the root cellar waiting for the time when she could afford to buy more sugar.

Because of the many foods that were in short supply, prices were going higher and higher. Farmers were urged to plant navy beans as a salable food crop.

"If everyone in the valley plants beans, maybe a carload can be sent to market in the fall," Mr. Cass said.

Father plowed some of the Roberts's land across the road from our house and planted the beans and some speltz a grain new to our area. He hoped this would be a good poultry food. Meat prices were high. Father built more nest boxes so we could set more hens and raise more poultry. Mother bought turkey and goose eggs for us to put under the setting hens too.

"Now the crops are in, and before haying time, I have two projects I intend doing something about," said Father in late May. "I'm going to dig us a well so we'll have a water supply, and I'm going to put a dam in the draw south of the house so the stock will have a good water supply."

"Are you going to try to put the well down all by yourself?" Mother asked.

"I got the cistern down, didn't I? Of course, I'll need some help after I get down a ways. I thought maybe I could hire Lenna and Verna O'Neill again," he said with a wink.

Ugh! I hated the thought of hauling up those heavy pails of dirt.

"Where will you dig?" Mother asked.

"I haven't decided. Do you have any suggestions?"

"Oh, yes. Why not have Dad Jahns twitch for the best spot?"

"My word! You don't believe in that, do you?" Father scoffed. "That's just plain silly."

"Of course, it's nonsense. But he offered. What can we lose?"

So, on a cloudy day the following week, we stood and watched Dad Jahns walk back and forth over the prairie near our house, arms akimbo, and his hands holding a forked willow branch.

"I really need a cherry tree fork, but I can't spare any from my orchard. Guess the willow will do," the old man said.

Mother explained the procedure to us. "Supposedly, if the point of the V turns downward, a well dug at that spot should have water."

Dad Jahns didn't want anyone walking with him. He needed to concentrate, he said. We watched from a distance and grew more and more tense as the forked stick dipped a little here or wobbled a little there. In the flash of an eye, the V turned downward.

"Oh ho," Dad Jahns exclaimed. He took a pointed stake from his pocket and marked the spot. Then he looked around, stared at the house and strode on, twisting his wrists to hold the stick horizontal again. The willow pointed down once more at a spot closer to the house.

"There you are. Dig there and you'll have water."

Father began digging as soon as Dad Jahns crossed the fields to his own house. By chore time, he had a waist-deep hole in the ground.

"It's surprising how much work I'm able to do these days without exhaustion," Father said at supper. "Dr. Thompson was right when he sent me to the outdoors."

The next day, I began helping Father at the well. He'd made a windlass. I turned the handle that rolled the rope around the iron bar and hauled the bucket of dirt up. At the same time, the rope lowered another pail for Father to fill. Father rested a minute or two while one pail went up and the other went down. Sometimes the buckets of dirt and rocks were so heavy it took all my strength to turn the handle. Each time, I had to get the bucket all the way up. If I let it drop back, it would strike Father. I braced my feet against the growing pile of dirt and strained until I won.

"I'm always amazed at the depth of the good dirt here in the valley," Father said. "If water supply could be regulated, there is nothing that couldn't be grown here, I suspect. Some day, this land will be irrigated, and instead of dry prairies, there will be verdant fields. Wouldn't it be wonderful to have a fine fruit orchard and shade trees and rosebushes?"

Father didn't say, "like in Ireland," but I knew that was on his mind.

By the third day, Father was using a ladder to go down to dig. The digging was getting harder and harder through soggy clay and stone. The buckets Verna and I took turns pulling up were heavier and heavier. When Father climbed out at noon, he said, "Should get water soon. It's getting downright muddy down there, better put on my overshoes, before I go down again."

The pails full of mud got very heavy. I looked forward to the end of the digging.

Dinner over and overshoes on, Father started down the ladder and then cried, "We've struck water! There's water in the bottom."

Sure enough, when I crouched down and peered into the dark depths, the sky and I were reflected in a pool of water.

"I'm going to bail this water out and dig down a bit further to ensure a good flow from this shale I've come to. Haul up, Lenna, my girl!"

We were both excited, and we worked hard to finish the well.

"If only the water is good," Father said again and again.

The next morning we hauled up a pail full of brown water. My heart sank. The bitter taste confirmed it was alkaline. All our hard work had been for nothing.

"Well, I tried," said Father, discouraged. He began building a platform over the well. "Maybe by some miracle, a way will be discovered so this kind of water can be used someday. I'll fix it so pump and pipe could be installed."

"What a disappointment," Father said to Old Man Jahns over the phone.

"Well, I said there was water there. Can't ever guarantee the kind, you know," the old man said laconically.

Father wasn't defeated. If a well wasn't the answer to our water problem, maybe the dam Fred Cass had suggested would be.

When the alfalfa was cut and the early haying done, Father hitched Babe and Bet to the scraper, and with James Sykes's help, they began to build a dam in the low place down in the pasture. It took them many days to get the earthen mound blocking the valley the way it should, and Fred Cass helped them finish it. Old Man Jahns complained that they'd ruined the big water hole down by his place, cutting off all that water runoff when the fall and spring rains came, but the men continued building the dam.

"You'll see. There'll be the same amount of water there in the spring. The runoff that fills that hole is not from here. We've studied this out carefully," Father reassured him. "No sense making a dam unless it's big enough to hold a quantity of water. Otherwise, it will dry up just the way the water holes do."

Verna and I could hardly wait for the dam to fill up. Would it be like Sylvan Lake in the Black Hills? Would trees grow around it? We had only one real tree, a cottonwood, in all our eight hundred acres. Would the water be deep enough for swimming? If so, Max Walters had promised to come out from town to teach us to swim.

"It will take fall rains and winter snow to fill it. We will just have to wait until next spring to know," Father said. "We'll have to be patient."

It seemed we always had to be patient where water was concerned.

Chapter 42

The Little Tree

The Gurney seed catalog filled with pictures of peonies, hollyhocks, dahlias, and fruit trees in full blossom came in the mail. I fantasized about lush English gardens and resting in the shade of an apple tree. I pictured bushel baskets of apples and plums in the fall and asked Father if we could order some trees. "They wouldn't grow, my girl," said Father. "You couldn't water them enough in hot weather, and the winters are too cold. Look at Old Man Jahn's trees. All he can do is keep them alive with all his watering and tending. They haven't grown an inch since we've lived here."

"I wonder about those Russian olive trees John Cass was talking about. They say they grow in spite of everything and make a fine windbreak," Mother said. "We could plant a row along the fence by the road. What do you think?"

"We might try," Father said.

"I wish we could have pine trees or spruce, but they wouldn't live in this climate," Mother said.

"They grow in the Black Hills. And that's only twenty-some miles away," I said.

"But they grow at an elevation that is cooler than here," Father said. "If they could live on the hot prairies, the seeds from those mountain trees would have covered this land a thousand years ago."

I wasn't ready to give up. "Papa, there's an evergreen in a coulee up at the edge of the Roberts's land. It's little, but it's green. If it can grow up there by itself, why couldn't evergreens grow in our yard?"

Father's eyebrows shot up in surprise. "You'll have to show me. I imagine it's protected from winter winds and summer heat down in the coulee. If it isn't too big, maybe we could transplant it into our yard."

I forgot about the little evergreen for awhile, and then on an April day after a hard spring rain, Father said, "This is the weather to transplant your evergreen, Lenna. I'll hitch Doc to the stoneboat. If we can stay on sod, away from the slippery gumbo, we won't have any trouble."

Doc dragged the stoneboat over the water-logged sod to the spot I remembered. At the sight of the little tree, I was tempted to ask Father not to dig it up. It looked so green, so alive, so perfectly at home in the coulee. I was afraid we'd kill it in the moving.

"Beautiful," Father exclaimed. "Little cedar, you're going to a new home where you'll bring beauty to us all."

His talking to it as though it could understand reassured me. Father had a way with green things. All I knew about growing plants I had learned from him. I trusted him to move it safely.

"How do you know it's a cedar?" I asked.

He took up the spade and cut a circle in the soil around its trunk.

"See the red bark and the feathery needle clusters shaped like hands?" He inhaled. "And that fragrance—aah, that's cedar."

Father dug far enough out from the trunk to leave a large root-ball. I handed him the gunny sacks, and we wrapped the soil-covered roots to protect them from the air and sun. I drove Doc and the stoneboat up close, and we eased the orphan tree onto the sledge and covered it with more sacks.

Doc slowly pulled the stoneboat, and Father and I walked alongside, ready to pounce if the little tree moved. "This is a courageous little cedar," Father said. "How many years has it struggled here against perverse and destructive winds, the killing heat, the shattering cold? We'll never know."

"I think it will have a better chance of surviving if it is where we can protect it, water it, and love and enjoy it," I said.

Father nodded, but I could see from his faraway look that he was deep in thought. "You know, I could make a sermon about this tough little tree," he said. "It isn't just by chance it has survived. It was strong and sturdy to start with and has fought against adversity. It put out good roots, stood up straight, and lifted its branches to the sun in God's heavens. It didn't lean against the protecting side of the coulee and grow crooked or grow too fast and become weak. It stands up against many men who couldn't do so well. God has watched over it, and now we'll help." He turned his gaze from the horizon to me. "I'm glad you found it, Lenna."

The whole family came out to help us decide where to plant it. We chose a spot near the front gate. Father dug a large hole, and then I steadied the tree as he placed it and firmed the soil around the roots. He had mixed a little rotted manure with the top soil, and I poured pail after pail of water from the cistern, to settle the earth around the roots. Father spread a mulch of straw under the branches and out over the wet soil to keep the roots cool and moist.

A few days later, when Father saw me hauling water to the cedar, he said. "Now, Lenna, you mustn't worry about the tree. It will do all right. Lots of things are transplanted in this life and grow more beautiful because of it. I was transplanted from Ireland, you know, and I'm doing all right." His eyes twinkled.

The tree stayed green and fragrant, apparently unaware of its uprooting. The Russian olives arrived from the nursery, and we planted them across the front of the yard. When the ground was warm enough, I planted the flower seeds that had been ordered with the trees—not peonies or dahlias, which would never have survived the Wild West, but cornflowers, daisies, and poppies, all tough enough to thrive on the South Dakota prairie.

Chapter 43

Graduation

Lenna O'Neill

Mother gave my hand a reassuring squeeze and strode up to the organ at the front of the room. The banner we had prepared hung behind her. We girls had cut out red paper letters and pinned them on two sheets that Mother had sewn together. "Step by Step" and "May 28, 1921 Graduation" arched across one side, and "Not Finished—Just Begun" across the other. A giant red crepe paper bow hung in the middle, and below that the letters spelled, "Watch Us Climb." Red hothouse roses, our class flower, stood a little limp but fragrant in a glass vase on the organ.

The first chords of a celebratory march rang in the packed schoolhouse. Parents and children squeezed into desks and lined the walls. For the first time, finishing eighth grade was being celebrated as an important accomplishment, and everyone in Provo wanted to be there to witness the big event.

Two weeks earlier, eight of us had gone through the grueling experience of taking the Fall River County eighth-grade examinations.

"I've taught these children for two years, and how they do in the exams reflects my ability to teach," Mother had fretted. "If some of those youngsters fail, they'll never go farther in school. Some won't anyway, but I want them to feel they've achieved something important."

"They'll feel important enough with all this fuss you're making about their graduation program," Father had said.

We had all struggled with the exams, but each of us felt, I'm sure, that we were doing our best for Mother's sake, as well as our own. I knew we'd all passed, because I'd rolled the diplomas myself and tied them with a red ribbon.

Just before the ceremony, Mother pinned a small red ribbon bow on each boy's lapel and each girl's dress. "To carry out the color scheme," she said, "but most of all to tell you I'm proud of you."

Accompanied by Mother's rousing march, we filed up the center aisle to the platform. At the final chord, we sat down in unison on a row of folding chairs, and the program began.

Mother thanked the people for coming and introduced us. All of us girls were wearing white—right down to our stockings and shoes. Mine was a ruffled dress Mother had made over from one of Aunt Harriet's Paris gowns. I'd wrapped my long hair in rags for two days to curl it, and Mother had pinned a large red velvet bow at the nape of my neck. When she announced my name, I felt as pretty as I ever had.

After the introductions, Mother told the people how proud of us she was. She talked about the importance of education. "But education isn't everything," she said. To be God-fearing, loving, honest, and determined to do your best is just as important."

Father, wearing the suit from the missionary box that Mother had tailored to fit, nodded in approval. Verna, Dorothy, and Roy sat beside him in the front row of desks. Verna wore a lacy, white dress Mother made to match her own. Even little Dorothy had a new outfit and curls for the occasion.

"These young people have lived up to my expectations in all respects," Mother concluded. "They deserve your praise, support, and guidance in whatever lies ahead for each of them. I shall follow their progress with interest and love."

Dottie came next. She was the salutatorian and, true to form, had her speech memorized before I even wrote mine. Every one of us had a little speech to make—on the class motto, flower, history, and so on.

The closer it came to my turn, the hotter I felt. My heart raced at the thought of presenting the valedictorian speech.

I'd known all these people for two years now and some of them for much longer, but I still felt shy and worried about forgetting the words. Mother wanted everything to be perfect, and the thought of disappointing her paralyzed me.

As I rose to the podium, I thought of how proud Mother was of me, and suddenly, I felt calm. Hours of telling my speech to Duke and Fanny as we herded the cattle had paid off. I looked out over the schoolroom crowded with the faces of all the people I'd come to care so deeply for. My words flowed clearly, distinctly, and "with meaning," as Mother had instructed.

After my speech, we filed by Mr. Soley, who gave us our certificates, and Mother, who handed each of us a long-stemmed red rose. "Congratulations," she said, her eyes shining as she shook our hands.

Chapter 44

Duke

The day after graduation, I went to bring in the cows for the night with Duke and Fanny. A few of them appeared from the next fold of the prairie, heading out by themselves. That draw had rocky sides with one place named Rattlesnake Ledge named for all the rattlers there. A prairie dog town populated the flats nearby. The prairie dogs were gay, sassy creatures, but the burrows were treacherous for horses' hoofs.

"Stay away from that place," Father had ordered, "If ever the cows are in there, send Fanny after them. You stay away."

The draw was deep and wide and full of rich grass. The year before, Father had cut hay there, but he'd also killed a five-foot-long rattler with a twelve-button rattle—the largest we'd ever seen.

"Go get them," I called to Fanny, and she darted away. Soon she had all the cows out of the draw and heading toward home. Duke and I followed close behind. My mind wandered, combing over the details of our graduation ceremony. I pondered on the importance of this threshold in my life.

"When you're through eighth grade, you're no longer a child," Mother had admonished us when we acted up in class. "People expect you to take responsibility and comport yourselves like young men and women."

"From now on, you're old enough to decide some things on your own," Father said when I'd asked him about which bridle I should put on Duke.

I was plunged deep in thought and totally unprepared for Duke's sudden leap to the side. He nearly threw me, and he trembled as I regained my seat and fumbled for the stirrup. My eyes searched the ground and landed on a coiled rattler.

I reflexively reviewed what Mother and Father had told me all my life: "Leave rattlesnakes alone. Just keep a safe distance and let it go its way. Leave them alone, and they'll leave you alone. You're too young to battle a rattlesnake."

Now I was no longer too young to kill a snake. I was an eighth-grade graduate. Father had said I was old enough to make some of my own decisions, hadn't he?

I looked around for stones or dirt clods to throw but couldn't find any. As I sought a weapon, the snake uncoiled and began to slowly slip away. How I wished I had Dad Jahns's snake stick, the long wire whip with the metal burrs at the end.

I got down from the saddle and unsnapped a rein, thankful I'd chosen the bridle with the extra-long reins. Wielding the rein like a whip, I took a step toward the snake. It saw me and coiled again. Its rattle blurred with the speed of its shaking.

I flung my arm back and struck with the rein. The metal snap fell short, and the rattler's head dove at the rein. I jerked it back. The snake moved closer. Its black eyes remained fixed on me. Its head hovered above its undulating coils, knotting for another strike.

The snap fell with a sharp blow full on the snake's body. It coiled tighter. Its tongue flicked and the rattle buzzed angrily.

The snake struck again and again, and so did I. The rein cut the air, and the metal snap struck the snake with each throw.

My heart raced but not from fear. I knew I could kill the snake. Fanny joined the battle. I didn't fear for her either. Her last tussle with a rattler had left her immune to the venom. She had lain more dead than alive for a week with her head swollen as big as her body. The swelling got so great her skin burst, exposing raw, red flesh at her throat. The snake that almost killed her had gotten away. This one wouldn't. I struck again. *That's for Fanny.*

Fanny pounced on the rattler, shook it hard, and flung it away.

"Fanny! Stop!" She stared at me and cocked her head. I ran to the snake, and before it coiled, I beat it with the metal end of the strap again and again. *That's for old Doc whose leg swelled to twice its size when he stepped on a rattler at plowing time.* Whap! *And that's for Mr. Howell's brown mule who suffocated after you bit its nose from your hiding place in the long grass.* Whap! *And this is for the time you coiled beneath Mother's skirt in the harvest field and scared us all to distraction.*

Fanny yapped, wild with excitement, and tried again to get at the snake, but she held back, wary of the cutting blows of the strap. Hot tears washed my cheeks. I screamed at my opponent in the grass as the metal snap landed its blows. The rattler stopped moving. Fanny's yapping turned into a high whine.

I held the rein back and focused hard to discern the slightest movement of the long, fat body in the grass. Fanny saw her chance and lunged for the snake. She tossed it away, then ran to it and took it in her mouth and threw it again.

"Stop it, Fanny!" I ran to the limp body sagging over sagebrush and kicked it off. It fell with a thud, exposing its white belly. I stomped on its head with my heel and ground it into the hardpan. "I've killed you!" I screamed. "I've killed you!"

Fanny slumped down on the ground panting, watchful for any signs of life in the rattler. I wiped the sweat and tears off my face with my sleeve. My heart pounded against my ribs.

Everyone who killed a rattler took the rattles to prove the age and size of the kill, but I had no knife. I doubted I could bear to touch the dead snake, but when I counted six rattles with the button, pride got the better of fear.

I walked back to Duke, snapped the rein back on to the bridle, and led him to the snake. He held his head low and blew a bit when we got near, but when I dropped the reins, he stood steady, as always. My stomach lurched as I lifted the snake with a forked branch of dead sagebrush. I grabbed hold of its hard, scale-like tail with one hand and draped it over Duke's back behind the saddle.

"Steady, Duke," I said, and tied the saddle-bag thongs around the limp body. I made sure the head touched only the saddle skirt in case some venom still clung. In the cooling air, as the sun reached the horizon, I urged Duke into a lope. The snake's body flopped with the motion of Duke's gait. A faint rattling of its tail accompanied us home.

Father met me in the yard, milk pail in hand. "Where in the world—" And then he saw the snake. "My goodness, girl!"

"I killed me a rattler, Papa!" Relief mingled with a sense of triumph, and tears threatened to spill over, but I held back. "I used the bridle rein!"

"You what? The bridle rein! Are you out of your mind? You could have been killed!" Father put down the milk pail and strode over to me. He might have seen the trembling of my lips when he said, more gently, "Get down, child."

He took a closer look at the rattler. "I should be cross with you, for you had us worried, and you disobeyed, but I suppose—well, it's done, and you were fortunate." He untied the thongs and lifted the snake off the saddle. "Hmmm. Not an extra big one, but six rattles. Not bad. I'll cut those for you later. You'll have a tale to tell over those."

I unsaddled Duke, slipped off the bridle, and turned him out to pasture. Father called after me. "Must have been quite a sight. A young lady with hair in long curls beating a rattlesnake to death." Yes, I thought. I must have been quite a fine sight.

Chapter 45

Daisy

Mother arranged a high school home-study program for me, but I had to appear in class in Edgemont every six weeks for exams. As the end of the first period drew near, Mother and I spent long evenings at the dining room table as she drilled me on Latin, algebra, English, and geography. When the time came for my first exams, an early winter snow and a bitter blast of cold air swept down on us.

Father wandered in from his study. "How are we going to get you into town for those tests?" he said. "I thought you could take the car, but this snow ends that plan. Even if you could get through, the radiator would freeze while you were in school."

"Maybe I could ride Duke," I suggested. In my heart, I knew I'd just as soon not go at all. I didn't know anyone at the high school except Elsie Stalford, and she was much older.

"Where would you put him when you got there?" Father asked. "There's no barn at the school. The poor horse would suffer out in the open, tied up in this kind of weather. I'll not have it."

The wind hammered the house, and sharp, fine snow sifted down the west windowpanes. Adolph came in to warm himself by the stove, and Father mentioned my dilemma. "You can take Daisy. That horse already has such a thick coat the cold doesn't faze her, and she'll get you there and back as fast as any horse around. With those barrel lungs, she never tires."

We'd had a fairly dramatic introduction to Daisy the previous New Year's Day, when Adolph had ridden into the yard with one of our other hands, Andy. "Look at the Christmas present I gave myself," he'd said. We were still living in the little house at the time, and we all came out to see what Adolph brought back from Yankton.

The horse was a shaggy black mustang, short but powerful looking. It looked like a sturdy yearling colt, but that morning, she'd fidgeted and pawed at the frozen ground, rolling her eyes. She'd left no doubt that she was a full-grown, fiery, and impatient horse. Adolph had glowed with pride as he put her through her paces, riding back and forth before our doorway. The horse pranced, tossed her head, chewed her bit, and would have bolted out of the yard if Adolph hadn't held her in. We girls clapped and shouted each time Adolph brought her past us, her long tail flying and her neck bowed with the urgency of her desire to run free. The thought crossed my mind that someday I would get Adolph to let me ride her.

"What a beauty! What's her name, Adolph?" shouted Verna.

"She's a daisy, all right. I think I'll call her Daisy." Adolph wheeled her in by Andy's horse, but a bit too close. Andy's horse reared.

I heard Mother shriek behind me. She was standing just inside the lean-to when a hoof broke through the roof right over her head!

Bits of wood flew every way, and dust settled down over the biscuits she had been making. Andy got thrown and Adolph dismounted. The two raced into the house and shamefacedly surveyed the damage.

"Oh, Mrs. O'Neill, I'm so sorry. Are you all right?" Andy said.

The young men apologized again and again, and began to pick up the splinters of wood and bits of tar paper that had come down.

"It just shows what a shack this place really is!" Mother said, still shaken. "It's a good thing we're about to move into a new house."

Since then, Mother had easily forgiven Daisy, and now, it seemed, I might finally have my chance to ride her.

The next morning, Adolph's wild pony and I left for town long before Mother started to school in Provo. The wind hadn't let up, and in the gray dawn, sugar-fine snow drifted across the ruts of the road ahead of me. Daisy was eager and sure-footed, and loped along at a steady gait. I was bundled up with as much clothing as I could wear comfortably. Only my eyes showed from beneath a scarf wound over my cap and across my face. The cold grew more penetrating as we headed into the wind, but I got used to it, and the exercise of riding kept me warm. Only my hands and feet took the brunt of the chill.

At the hogbacks, I welcomed the momentary shelter from the wind and knew the worst was over. I checked to see if my books were secure in their bag at the back of the saddle, looked at the lunch bag tied on the other side, and let Daisy have her head. The level road at Craven Flats and the wind at our backs made the going easier.

From there, it took little time to reach the final hill before Edgemont. The wind turned colder when I got into town. There was no fence around the schoolyard, and I struggled to see through the snow, blowing off the icy field like steam. The flag pole on the south side of the building presented itself as the only possible hitching post for Daisy. I hoped the building might offer some protection from the wind.

I slid down onto feet wooden with cold and took off her bridle with stiff, aching fingers. "No use in her having to keep that cold metal in her mouth all day," Adolph had said. I snapped one rein into the ring of the halter and tied the end around the flagpole. He'd told me to loosen the girth too but to leave the saddle on to help keep her warm.

I hooked the bridle over the saddle horn, untied my saddle bags, and watched Daisy rearrange her position until her tail faced the wind. Reluctant to leave her, and even more hesitant about going into the classroom filled with strangers, I crossed the yard and entered the imposing building.

I endured the morning classes in silence. The tests didn't give me any trouble, but my shyness and self-consciousness almost made me ill. At the noon break, I expected to be the only one left behind as the others went home for dinner. To my surprise, a girl who introduced herself as Bonnie Langly led me to a room with a big stove. A black girl, the first I had ever seen, sat by the fenders, warming her feet. She asked my name and said hers was Thelma. Bonnie and I dragged crates over and unpacked our dinners.

"I live in the country too," Bonnie said, "but Father is a barber, and I stay in town with him during the week. My brothers stay home with my mother and go to the Hudson School. We live in the small white house you pass right after you cross the hogbacks."

"I went to Hudson School too," said Thelma. "My brothers and sisters go there now. We live a long way west of Bonnie's house, though."

I felt better after the friendly conversation and the warmth. When I returned to the classroom, I had two friends and knew my way around the building. I had survived the morning and felt pretty good about my first day of high school. Then came Latin class. Everyone except me seemed to know all the answers to the teacher's review questions. I didn't know most of the answers and became embarrassed and confused, suffering a new agony every time the teacher called my name.

As I took the Latin test, I realized I didn't know my vocabulary well enough, and I had difficulty with the conjugations. I answered the questions I could and sat nervous and miserable until the end of the period. When the teacher reviewed my exam, she looked over her glasses at me and said nothing.

English, the last class of the day, went much better. I liked the teacher, Miss Warnock, and had little problem writing the answers to the questions she put on the chalkboard. Miss Warnock saw that I was through, and that I had been craning my neck to check on Daisy.

She came over to me and asked in a loud whisper, "Is that your pony out there?"

I nodded.

"I've been wondering all day whose it was. Aren't you afraid it's cold?"

I nodded again.

"How far did you come?"

"About eight miles."

"All that way! Say, you'd better get started if you're going home today."

I didn't need urging. I'd been hearing the clanking of the chain on the pole as Daisy tossed her head and pulled on the halter rein. I knew she was cold and as anxious to go home as I was. I pushed my books and thermos into the sack and walked as quietly as possible down the squeaky stairs to the door.

Daisy blew loudly through her cold nose when she saw me coming and pawed the ground eagerly. I remembered what Father had told me about warming the bit before putting the bridle back on. I had seen him warm bits in his hands, but this bit was so cold, I didn't think my hands would warm it. I opened my coat and put it under my arm. That must have worked, because Daisy didn't object when I slipped it into her mouth. I put the bridle over her ears and fastened the throat latch.

Daisy danced with eagerness to go. She started away at a dead run. There was no holding her. Never before had I ridden a horse this fast. I forgot everything that had troubled me and gloried in the strength and speed of the little horse.

We were up Skene Hill and well along toward the hogbacks before she really settled down. I loved racing with the wind, but we had miles to go, and I pulled her in to conserve her strength. She began a long-striding trot, still eager and strong, and we moved along quickly. Once over the hogbacks, she wanted to lope again, and I let her out. The wind at our backs lessened as the sun lowered in the metallic sky. The cold began to penetrate, and I pulled the scarf tighter over my ears and around my neck.

I was so muffled up; I didn't hear the hoofbeats behind me until Daisy pricked up her ears. I turned to see a man on a tall bay approaching fast. Pretending not to notice, I kept

Daisy in her steady swift gait. The Wyoming border was not far ahead, and the stories about outlaws who hid out just beyond it ran through my mind.

The man pulled up beside us. "Hi!"

"Hi," I said, trying not to betray my extreme discomfort.

"Been following you a ways. That's quite a little mustang you've got there." He sounded friendly enough. "And she's not even blowing. How far did you come?"

"From Edgemont," I answered politely. Mother had warned me long ago never to talk to strangers, but it seemed a little silly, since we were riding beside each other, and there was no one else on the whole wide prairie.

"Pretty cold," he said, and I agreed.

We rode in silence for a while.

"You going to Provo?" he asked.

"No, I live over the hill." I urged Daisy into a lope.

"Better not wear out that little black beauty, sis." He looked at me almost crossly over the steam of his breath in the frosty air. "Beats me what you're doing out here in the cold."

I was glad to reach the "Y" in the road where the ruts leading to our house cut down through the Roberts land.

He raised his gloved hand in farewell, and he loped away toward Provo. He and his horse looked big and dark against the early winter sunset.

When we were home, I unsaddled and fed Daisy and gave her neck a pat of thanks. Before leaving the barn, I threw down some fodder for the cows, my usual outdoor chore this time of day. It felt good to be home in time to do what I was supposed to do. The cows steaming in their cold stanchions seemed glad I was home too.

Mother and Verna greeted me happily. "I hoped you would be here soon," Mother said. "How were the tests?"

She pulled a chair up to the stove. "Put your feet in the oven, child. You must be frozen."

"No. It wasn't so cold coming home, and Daisy just flew. She's the nicest horse," I gushed. "I love to ride her. Of course, she's not as smart as Duke, but she's surely a fine little horse." I would have gone on to avoid talking about school, but she interrupted me.

"But what about school? Were the tests hard?"

There was no putting it off. I had to tell Mother about the Latin.

"Don't worry about it. Maybe you know more than you think you did. We'll just work harder on the memorizing this next six weeks."

I knew Mother was disappointed, but she wouldn't say anything to discourage me. She understood my humiliation. I promised myself I would do better and changed the subject, telling her about the man on the bay horse.

Mother caught her breath. "I never thought about anything like that happening. Well, you acted like a lady, and that's what matters. I wonder who it was." Her voice drifted off and she began preparations for supper.

"Well, it couldn't have been Prince Charming. He rides a white horse," Verna said flippantly. I imagined she was a little jealous of me and my day full of adventures. My feet warmed through in the oven, and in the comfort and safety of my mother's kitchen, my tiredness melted away.

Chapter 46

Vacation

(left to right) Verna and Lenna O'Neill

G et Mama! Get Mama!" Father cried. Verna lay limp in his arms. He was running across the yard from the barn, and I dropped my pail and raced past him.

I screamed for Mother at the door and turned back to help Father get Verna inside. The sight of her gray face filled me with terror. Mother dashed in from the kitchen. The flash of fear in her eyes disappeared as she took charge.

"Put her on our bed. What happened?"

"I don't know. We were in the middle of milking, when I looked up and saw Birdie tearing around the corral with Verna dangling underneath her. Her hair was caught in the heifer's poke." Father kneeled down next to the bed. "Oh, my darling, where does it hurt?"

Verna moaned, and her eyes opened to narrow slits. Mother got a washcloth and a pan of water and wiped Verna's dirty, tear-stained face.

"Can you move?" Mother said, betraying no emotion, sounding gentle but clinical, like Dr. Thompson. "Try moving your legs. Where does it hurt? Can you roll over?"

Verna just moaned and cried. She couldn't answer Mother's questions except with a nod or a slight shake of her head.

"I'm going to take off your clothes now to see if you're hurt anywhere else," Mother said. "Joe, help her sit up."

Verna cried out when Father put his arm around her and propped her up. Dorothy and Roy hovered at the end of the bed, fingers in their mouths, eyes wide open.

"No great damage done," Mother said. Three hoofprints on your back, and a hank of hair pulled out on the top of your head. You're lucky and should thank the Lord in your prayers. Now stop crying and tell us what happened."

Verna stopped her hysterics on Mother's command. "Birdie was lying down chewing her cud, and I leaned over to see about a lump on her neck. She jerked up and the poke went through my hair." She touched the top of her head and winced. "I couldn't get loose. I don't remember the rest."

"That heifer tore around the corral three times with half the cows stampeding with her before that poke straightened out and set Verna free. It's a wonder her back isn't broken." Father's face was strained and white. "I'll get rid of that cow. She doesn't respect fences, and she's not going to be a good milker, and now this—"

"Now, Joe. Don't be rash," Mother said. "You're going to stay put in bed until you feel better, Verna."

"I'm all right. I can't be sick. We're going to Denver!"

Mother and Father had promised us a trip to Denver once Verna graduated. We were scheduled to leave on the train in two days. I had been looking forward to it, but not nearly as much as Verna. She always looked ahead with enthusiasm and was plunged into black despair if things didn't work out the way she had planned. She had talked about the Denver trip incessantly. Her bag was packed before the rest of us even thought over what we would take. Ordinarily, she was a sleepyhead, but in her excitement, she woke up early and cheerfully. She rushed through her chores, singing at the top of her voice while she worked. One day, Mother, Father, and I had been delayed in town past milking time, and Verna milked all twenty-three cows before we got home. The rest of the family made jokes about her sudden streak of ambition, but Verna paid us no mind.

Though her spirit wanted to move her off the bed, she cried out when she tried to get up. For that evening, Verna surrendered to her wounds.

Father and I did the milking in silence. Even with Adolph and Tom at the table, a somber mood invaded our supper meal. Roy and Dorothy didn't understand, but the rest of us knew Verna might have been killed.

Two days later, we deposited Roy and Dorothy with the Stalfords and boarded the train to Denver. Verna wouldn't admit that she ached for fear she wouldn't get to go. She had purple hoof prints on her back, and Mother had to help her rearrange her hair so the raw spot on her scalp didn't show.

The overnight trip in a coach car tired Father and me. He suffered his usual insomnia, and I was too excited to sleep. When we reached Denver, we went to our hotel, washed up, and though it was noon, went to bed for awhile.

Sally Sykes was with us, and she and Verna and I shared a room adjoining our parents. We opened the windows to enjoy the mountain air after the cinders and fumes of the train. We girls quickly dropped off to sleep, but I was soon awakened when I felt Sally rise from the bed. To my astonishment, she picked up her white canvas slippers and tossed them out the window.

"Sally! What are you doing?"

She turned and gazed in my direction, unseeing. Then she blinked and raised her eyebrows in puzzlement. "I thought I was putting them in my closet at home."

We roused Father and he rushed down four flights of stairs and retrieved Sally's only pair of shoes from the gutter.

Sally's caper destroyed any hope of further napping. We all went down into the streets and strolled past the shop windows. We girls had never seen such huge buildings, rushing traffic, crowded sidewalks, and dazzling store-window displays. A policeman directed traffic at an intersection, and we stopped to stare at the novelty.

"If we should get separated or if anything at all frightening should happen, you ask a policeman for help," Mother said, hustling us past him. "They're here to help."

We walked for miles, or so it seemed. Verna was forever ahead or behind us, absorbed and curious. We stopped in front of a dress shop and Mother pointed at a saucy hat. "Verna, that would look so lovely on you." When we didn't hear Verna's characteristic glee, we turned and saw that she wasn't with us. Sally and I were about to retrace our steps in search of her, but Father stopped us. "Let her look for us. Then she'll learn to keep up."

We waited and waited, but she didn't come around the corner. At last, we turned back and found Verna approaching a policeman. When Father retrieved her and brought her back to us, her flushed cheeks betrayed her embarrassment. Father was right. It was the last time we had to go looking for her.

The next morning, we traveled by tourist limousine to Colorado Springs and toured the Garden of the Gods. We had our pictures taken with a burro in the shadow of one of the great red rocks. Though I loved the bustle and all the sights of Denver, the respite returned a familiar sense of peace to my spirits.

We were all tired and beginning to think of home when we got back to our hotel, but we had several hours before our train was scheduled to leave for Provo.

"Do you suppose we could go to a moving picture show?" Mother asked. "There's a theater right around the corner."

Verna and I thought that was a wonderful idea. Mother had seen *The Birth of a Nation* advertised in *The Edgemont Enterprise* and had insisted that Verna and I go to see it, while Father took care of his business. Always anxious to broaden our horizons, she had persuaded Father to let us go. Enthralled, we watched the story unfold from the last row in the theater. To our dismay, Father tapped me on the shoulder before it was over. He insisted we had to leave before the end. I know Father felt there was some sort of wickedness involved in the movie business, and it made him uneasy to have us there.

This time, however, he didn't object, perhaps because in Denver, there was no one to criticize the preacher for going to the movies. Mother had read the book, and she assured him that *Shepherd of the Hills* was a fine, wholesome story.

The grandeur of the theater took my breath away. We settled in bright-red folding seats at the back of the theater. Plush red carpets ran down the aisle to the stage, and gold baroque trim embellished everything in sight. A mountain scene decorated the curtain, and when it rose, organ music swelled to a grand crescendo as the screen flickered to life.

Mother kicked off her shoes, and we all settled in the luxurious seats as darkness descended and the music ebbed. For almost two hours, we lived the story, spellbound, thrilling at the action and dissolving into tears at the bidding of the organ music.

"The End" appeared on the screen much too soon. I rubbed my eyes when the lights came up, and Mother struggled to stuff her swollen feet back into her shoes. Father checked his pocket watch and hustled us out of the magical world onto the street.

We hurried to the depot, just in time to board the train. As we rode east, the clicking rhythm of the train wheels beat the rhythm of "The Arkansas Traveler," which we had heard at the beginning of the movie. Mother and we girls hummed and sang snatches of the song. When Father contributed some of the words we couldn't recall, I knew he'd enjoyed the movie as much as we had.

We traveled through the night, and I noticed Mother grew quieter as the No. 44 carried us nearer to Provo.

In the hot, dry summer that followed, we often recalled the ice-cold drinking water in the city faucets, the coolness of the mountain air, and the beautiful things in the store windows. Mother talked more and more about the advantages of living where there were "cultural opportunities," a place where people were a part of "the modern world."

Chapter 47

This Terrible Land

The young crops curled in the searing heat. Father suffered with every sprout that struggled in the parched earth and watched the burning sky with great anxiety.

"The corn won't have a chance if it doesn't rain soon," he said. "This cruel climate doesn't give growing things a chance."

Father told me not to waste the cistern water, but I began watering the cedar tree early in the season—a full pail every night. My cosmos and marigolds along the walk probably wouldn't make it, but I watched over them and watered them a little too.

The incessant wind wore its way across the land day after day. At night, it continued to toss the weakened grain and wilting corn. Without a chance to cool, the earth hardened and cracked. Cattle had to forage farther and needed more water, but the waterline on the large water holes lowered, and the small holes dried completely. Bleached snail shells clung to the dying slough grass.

"There'll be no crops this year unless we have rain soon," Father said. "The oat is burned so badly, I wonder if it will even head out, and the corn is sad to behold."

Father despaired but went about his regular work. Tom and Adolph continued cultivating the corn, though their hopes of saving it dimmed.

At last, a heavy cloud bank rose at the horizon, and inside of an hour, a heavy downpour drenched the countryside. The limp grains and weakened blades of grass bent low before it. Rivulets of water ran along the cracks in the earth and stood in pools in the low places. The corn leaves rattled with the beating drops, then lifted higher with new strength. The cattle absorbed the cool wetness into their gaunt backs and rose to graze the freshened grass. We all breathed deeply of the clean, moist air and felt brave once more.

"What a blessing," Father said. "It's wonderful what water can do." His shoulders lifted. "Think I'll go to Hopper's for that young sow tomorrow. I don't look forward to hauling it in the wagon. Pigs are so unpredictable."

He was back by noon—without the pig.

"The stupid thing jumped out over the tailgate down by the tracks. I'll eat my lunch and then go back and bring it home on foot."

"I suppose you couldn't get it back in the wagon," Mother said. She obviously hadn't been listening. She was engrossed in cutting out a dress for Verna from the ripped and washed pieces of one of the Paris gowns.

"Of course not, or I wouldn't be going back for it," Father said irritably. "A grown hog isn't that easy to handle. We loaded it through a chute at Hopper's. That sow is about two hundred pounds of orneriness."

"But Joe, do you think you can herd it all the way up here? Why not get some help? You could send Lenna to get Adolph or Tom."

"They drive the things to market in Ireland. Guess I can handle one here."

We could see the pig rooting around in the weeds down along the edge of the railroad right-of-way and watched as Father walked down through the pasture in the breathless quiet of the steamy afternoon.

He fought the pig all afternoon, working it back and forth, gradually edging it toward home. The pig easily ducked under the barbed-wire fences, crossing from one side to the other, while Father climbed over the wires. The heat grew more suffocating as the late afternoon breezes died.

"Papa is wearing himself out," Mother said. "He's liable to have sunstroke in all this heat. Lenna, I know he said not to, but don't you think you should go help? At least go down there with some water."

I filled a jug and hurried to him. His face was red, and he was panting with the heat.

"Water! Is there anything better in the world!"

Together we drove the pig the rest of the way home. I feared Father might collapse as we herded the creature into the pig lot, but he went about doing the chores, and it wasn't until suppertime that he complained about a headache.

"I'll never, ever try to drive a pig anywhere again," he said. "Either those Irish women who drive theirs to market have more patience than I, or they have a secret method."

Hours later, Mother shook me awake from a deep sleep.

"Lenna," she said in an urgent whisper. "Come at once. I need you."

I rushed down the stairs to my parents' bedroom, where I found Father tossing wildly in their bed. Mother bent over him, trying to hold him still and wiped his face with a wet cloth.

"He's having chills and is out of his head. Stay with him, while I get more covers and water for the hot-water bottle."

I threw my arms across him, but Father struggled against me. I felt the sharp bones of his thin, shaking body beneath me. His sunburned face turned from side to side above the patchwork quilt. He moaned and talked nonsense through chattering teeth.

When Mother returned, she said, "I called Dr. Thompson. He says Papa has sunstroke. We must keep him warm and give him liquids when he is able to drink. When the chilling stops, I'm to use cold compresses on his brow and neck."

Several hours later, Father quieted. Mother made him drink two glasses of water, pulled the covers up to his chin, and put another cool compress on his forehead. When I rose to go back to bed, she put her arm around me. "I was so frightened."

"I know, Mother. So was I."

"Papa is wearing himself out. I sometimes wonder if he'd be any worse off back in the ministry."

"Try to get some rest, Mother. You worry so much over him."

Mother managed a wan smile, and her voice cheered a bit. "You are such a comfort to us, Lenna. I knew I could waken you, and you would know what to do to help. Thank you, dear daughter."

A week later, hail roared out of the west, ripped the leaves off the young corn, beat the wheat into a soggy mass in muddy fields, drove cattle into fences, and knocked holes in the roofs over people's heads. Gardens were decimated, chickens hammered to death. The corn and grain, the seed, the fodder—all were all gone. Only the prairie grass, beaten and broken, would survive. It would rise again, the only thing left for winter feeding.

Father cut hay in every little draw that had grass. He gleaned every bit of grain that had somehow withstood the onslaught. He and other farmers took hogs and cattle to market and sold them at a loss in order to have less stock to feed. We could no longer afford to have Adolph and Tom work for us regularly. Verna and I took their place, hauling and stacking the hay and doing whatever else we could. Father borrowed at the bank for feed grains to take us through the winter.

"While you're borrowing, don't you think we should have a new car?" Mother said.

Father's head shot up. "A new car!"

"I know it sounds preposterous when things are so hard for us, but the Model T is wearing out. Now that I'll be teaching at the Hudson School, I'll have to have more reliable transportation. I'll have much farther to go, and the girls will be driving the car to school in Edgemont from there."

Father thought a moment. "You know, you're right. The car isn't too reliable anymore. I'll see what I can do." A rare smile crossed his lips. His spirits lifted no doubt at the thought of a new automobile.

"And, Joe, do find out exactly what we owe at the bank. We mustn't get in over our heads."

When Father drove into the yard with the new Model T sedan, his eyes twinkled with delight. We all piled in and he drove to Dad Jahns's corner on the section line and back.

"Thought I might as well get it now," he said, as we tooled down the lane. "I thought it was probably just right. What do you think?"

"I thought we'd find out how much we owed and then decide," Mother said. "Can we afford it? How much do we owe at the bank?"

Father passed through our gate and slowed to make a wide turn across the yard. "This ought to keep us warm in winter, and just listen to how quietly the engine runs. Got a good price for the old car too." He glided to a stop at the garage door, grand as the limousines in Denver.

We all scrambled out and stood around admiring our new automobile, except Father. He remained behind the wheel, holding on as if the Model T could shield him from Mother's insistent questioning.

"How much did it cost, Joe?" Mother asked again.

"Five hundred, but I got two hundred for the old car." He drove away from Mother into the old barn, which still served as our garage.

"My goodness," Mother said. "It's a good thing I'll be teaching."

After supper, Mother and Father stayed sitting at the table while Verna and I cleaned up the dishes. He spread out the papers that showed his transactions at the bank.

Mother added up some figures and gasped. "Eighteen thousand dollars!" She stared at Father. "This includes the seed grain for next spring, right?"

"No. That's what we owe with all the loans consolidated into one. We still have to borrow for seed. I was shocked too, Dearie, and I suggested to Mr. Payne that maybe we should sell more of the stock. But he said to wait and see how things are next spring."

Mother's voice rose to a wail. "Joe, how will we ever pay that much back?"

"The bank doesn't seem worried. A couple of good crops and we'll be all right again."

"I don't care whether they're worried or not. I'm worried! It might take us the rest of our lives to pay that off, with or without good crops."

"Calm down, Dearie. The Lord will provide. And worry won't help. We'll just do the best we can." Father put his arms around Mother and kissed her. I don't think he had ever seen her so discouraged, and I saw the care and worry in his face, much as he tried to hide it.

Chapter 48

Drought

Roy and Dorothy O'Neill

The teakettle sang on the oil stove at the old Gladson place, and I measured the tea into the tea ball, hung its chain over the lip of the teapot, and poured in the boiling water. Father slapped the dust from his clothes and washed up. He splashed cistern water from the blue basin onto his wind-burned face and pulled the dusty towel off the hook.

It was late July, 1923, and we were haying. Although the hay was as short and dry as fall timothy, we took what we could get. In the third year of drought, the wind and sun had scorched the prairies since early June. Across the road from our house on the home place, the corn had not even come up. Father checked a handful of the dry soil and found that the planted kernels of corn had not even sprouted. Any winter moisture in the ground had been whipped away by the searing winds, and none had fallen for almost two months. Anything growing in the spring had been struck down. The white, metallic sky held no clouds, no hint that rain might come at last.

"It hardly seems worth the effort," Father said. "Won't be more than two loads down there. Four years ago, there was a whole stack of hay taken from that draw." Father's voice broadcast his despair.

He wiped the dust from his glasses and put them back on. He sighed as he took a seat at the worn oak table in the abandoned house we used for noonday meals when we worked our fields at the Gladson place. He wore discouragement like a shabby cloak on his sloping shoulders. The lines in his face had deepened over the past three years, marring his once-handsome face. Father, the perfectionist, the dreamer, the lover of the land who had worried, worked, and prayed through the droughts could not keep his head held high through this one. I felt the weight of his defeat.

I spread a clean cloth over the table and set out the mismatched cups and the salt and sugar we stored in the rickety cupboard. With no hired men to feed, I no longer cooked a hot dinner. Verna had packed sandwiches for us that we carried in tin buckets.

I poured the tea and retrieved my sandwich from my pail. Father sat across from me, his eyes fixed on a letter lying on top of his sandwiches in his pail. I recognized Mother's firm, round handwriting. Why, I wondered, would she be writing to Father when only that morning she had seen us both? Father sighed deeply, laid the letter aside, and began eating his sandwich without much enthusiasm.

"Your mother has the will of—I don't know what." He blew the steam off his tea. "Drought or no drought, we can't move away now. We'd lose everything we've worked for all these years."

I stared at him, unbelieving. Move away? I thought back on snatches of conversation I'd heard and dismissed. Now, my parents' discussions about the drought and the debts took on a new meaning that left me cold and afraid.

"We wouldn't move away, would we, Papa?" I had hardly enough breath to get the words out.

"I hope not. But these are awful times, and Mama thinks we have no choice. Don't worry about it. We shall see."

I cleaned our cups and wiped out the lunch buckets.

"As soon as you're ready, let's finish up this job." His voice sounded muffled with sadness.

At home that evening, Father went doggedly about doing the chores. I fed the chickens and helped with the milking. When we went to the house for supper, I noticed that Father and Mother avoided each other's eyes and spoke hardly at all. The ache inside me was almost unbearable.

At supper, however, Mother broke her silence.

"A man by the name of Pease from the Federal Reserve bank in Omaha was here today. He said they are examining all accounts of the Edgemont Bank. He wanted a list of everything we own. They need security on our loans."

Father just shook his head and picked at his food.

"He even wanted to know the amount of our cream checks. I disliked him at once. All he can think of is money. I'm frightened, Joe. If we can't make some sort of payment, they're liable to come and take everything away from us."

Father looked sharply at Mother. "Don't be too quick to judge. Checking on securities is his business, and we haven't been able to make payments on our loans for some time. I imagine the bank is burdened these days with people like us who can't pay their debts. But the authorities will just have to be patient as long as there are no crops to sell."

"There's only one thing to do, and why can't you see it?" Mother burst out. "You can answer that call in DeSmet, and we can turn everything over to the bank and go back East." She slammed down her fork and knife. "I'm tired of grubbing for a living out here on the prairie. Our children need a chance at the better things in life. You're needed in the ministry more than you're needed out here."

Father gazed at his plate, unwilling to look at Mother.

"Oh, Joe. Can't you see? There's only one thing to do. You're a fine preacher. Let us go back to civilization. We're not defeated. We're being wise."

Verna and I sat still as death, barely breathing. I couldn't believe I was hearing these words from Mother.

She lowered her voice, which only served to heighten the fearful impact. "I meant what I said in the note. If you won't do it, I will. I'm an ordained minister, and I'll answer that call. The children and I will go without you."

Tears started in Mother's eyes, but she remained steadfast, sitting ramrod straight and formidable before my father.

The blood drained from Father's face. "Oh, Dearie, no," he said, his voice as broken as his heart. Without another word, he rose from the table and left the house.

Roy and Dorothy clamored for their food. Mother said a short blessing, and we tried to eat. Verna and I were on the edge of tears. Father's chair stood empty. I cast an accusing glance at Mother, but seeing the pain in her face, I turned my eyes to my plate and moved my food around with my fork.

"What are we going to do? Are we moving away forever?" Verna asked, her eyes wide with apprehension.

Mother ignored her and talked more to herself, it seemed, than to us. "We can't stay here if we can't pay our debts, and we owe so much money after these crop failures. It would take years and years and years to pay it all back. We just can't spend the rest of our lives paying our money to that bank."

She broke off abruptly and directed Verna to pour Roy some more milk. Even in her anxious state, she didn't miss a thing.

"We're so isolated here," she went on. "I sometimes have the feeling the rest of the world has gone on and left the people of this valley behind. If we stay here, you girls will never have a chance for a really good education, or a taste of the gentler, good things of life."

Verna and I kept our eyes on our plates. We didn't dare comment or ask any questions, though I was burning to know what had driven Mother to threaten Father like that.

Then, as if I had spoken out loud, Mother explained. "I took the bull by the horns a few weeks ago and wrote to the state superintendent of the Congregational Church and told him Papa's health had returned, and we felt we should be back in the ministry. A letter came right back saying a minister was needed in DeSmet—that's clear across the state near the Minnesota border—and would Papa be interested in candidating on the first Sunday in August."

Dorothy and Roy fidgeted in their seats, and Mother excused them from the table.

"When I showed Papa the letter, he was angry and said I had gone behind his back. Well, maybe I did, and I feel bad about that, but how else could I get him to consider it? He won't answer the letter or let me answer it. It's been ten days, and today I put a note in Papa's lunch pail with an ultimatum. Either he preaches there as a candidate, or I will."

Mother's eyes flashed, but her lips trembled. I didn't know what to say, and Verna looked as dumbfounded as I did.

"He has to decide tonight. Tomorrow, I'm going to send the letter. If I don't, it will be too late."

Father didn't come in again before we children went to bed. I caught a glimpse of him sitting on the back steps staring off into the clear night. Fanny lay beside him, her head resting on his leg. As I trudged up the stairs to bed, I longed to be out there, under the stars, comforting him.

Chapter 49

Decision

(left to right) Lenna and Verna O'Neill

Mother won. Father thought it best not to discuss our decision to leave with anyone outside the family for the present. He had to tell Fred Cass, because we needed Eric's help with the grain cutting. After Father explained why we needed Eric, the Casses came over to see us that same evening.

"There's no reason to panic," Fred said.

The grownups were sitting in the parlor. Verna and I loitered in the background.

"Sure, we've had some bad years, but the land always comes back," Fred said. "There's a great future here on this last frontier. One good crop and we'll all be back on our feet. If you go now, you'll lose all you've accomplished in these last nine years."

"No, we won't," Mother said. "Joe has his health back, our children have grown strong and healthy, and we have wonderful friends like you. If we stay, there is little ahead but grinding work and struggle. Joe is a good preacher and should do the Lord's work now that he is well again. Besides, we need to be thinking of the education and future of our children."

"It's true, Fred," Father said. "It's a hard choice to make, but I've prayed about it and thought it out. I've learned to love this land, harsh as it is. I could stay here the rest of my days, close to the soil, enduring this hard climate, and I'd be content with God and man. But it wouldn't be fair to my family. There is beauty and knowledge that should be a part of their lives, and I can't give them that if we stay here."

"What's more beautiful than a prairie sunset, a fine horse, a field of golden wheat?" Fred exclaimed. "And aren't you doing God's work right here in this community? You've helped us all so much. How can you think of deserting us?"

I slipped away, feeling that I couldn't bear to hear another word from Father and Mother. Out on the back step, where Father had thought it all out those few nights ago, I sat with my arm draped over Fanny and wept into her black and white coat.

The red morning sun glinted off Adolph's new shiny black car when he came to pick up Father the next morning. Father had arranged to ride with him in his brand-new Overland car. Adolph had given up his homestead and was returning to Yankton to marry his sweetheart.

"If you move to DeSmet," he said, "we'll be in the same general area of the state, and we'll be seeing each other again. It's just so long, for now."

I clung to that little shred of happiness as he and Father drove away.

Eric rode up on his horse just as the Overland turned the corner at Dad Jahns's and disappeared. Father had asked if I could ride the reaper while Eric drove the tractor, and I'd said I could, even though I'd never done it before. I'd looked forward to spending a few days working in the fields with Eric. Seeing him now lessened my despair.

We harvested the oats in the fields near home first. I rode the binder, and with my foot on a pedal, tripped the bundles off the machine's platform at spaced intervals. They lay in my wake in windrows, ready for shocking. When the twine broke, or something stuck in the sickle, I yelled for Eric, and he'd stop the tractor and set things right again.

Eric took care of the machines and went about the work with the wisdom of a grown man. It was hot and dusty on the binder, and my eyes and nose bothered me, but I was a good hand and held up my end of the job.

Eric and I were a bit self-conscious around each other. He'd been my beau since that first week at the Provo school, giving me little gifts and seeking me out at social affairs. I'd always taken him for granted and acted unimpressed, but I was touched by his devotion.

Eric and I worked furiously to get the grain harvested before Father got home. We finished the last of it on Monday afternoon, happy that the grain seemed to be a little heavier than Father had estimated.

Father was home when Eric and I pulled into the yard with the tractor and binder. I felt proud and grown up when I told him how much Eric and I had accomplished.

"If the rest of the grain is this much better than you thought, maybe we won't have to move," I said hopefully.

Father just smiled and went in the house with Mother and the little ones hanging on his arms and Verna happily skipping alongside.

My thin thread of hope lasted only a few days. Father was asked to lead the church in DeSmet and accepted the call. When the letter arrived, I dashed to the barn, saddled Duke, and rode away from the house with Fanny racing beside me.

I was inconsolable, thinking only of being torn away from everything I loved—beloved Duke with whom I had raced across the prairie and brave Fanny, my constant and dutiful shadow. I wondered how many more times Duke and I would be flying like this. What would happen to him? Would he be sold? Would other people be kind to him and understand his quirky ways? Would they be patient when he spooked at silly things like rabbits? My tears flowed afresh.

A stone lay on my heart as I thought of the broad land with the glowing cactus flowers, the fossil rocks, the meadowlarks, the sunsets, the roaring, sweeping summer storms and winter blizzards. The rosebush I had ordered that spring from the catalog was living and green in spite of the drought, and now, I must leave it to die.

Duke trotted into the draw at the bottom of our land and stirred up the fragrance of the sweet mint growing in the grass. The cows grazed on the slope above us. Seeing the fat, orange sun hovering on the horizon, I whistled to Fanny. She raced up the hill after them, her tail flying like a giant feather, and helped me herd them home.

Chapter 50

Farewell

(front row, left to right) Joseph O'Neill, Dora O'Neill,
Roy O'Neill, and Dorothy O'Neill; (back row, left to right)
Verna O'Neill and Lenna O'Neill

Eric stood in the middle of the yard, hands on his hips. I could tell from his stance that something wasn't right.

"They took the organ and the cook stove, Mrs. O'Neill," he blurted the moment we got out of the car.

"Took the organ and the range?" Mother cried. "Who? When?"

We rushed into the house. Sure enough. They were gone.

"Doctor Thompson came out, and when he found you had gone, he sent out some men with a truck and they carried those things out of the house. I'm just sick about it, Mrs. O'Neill."

"Don't worry, Eric. I'm sure you did what you could," Father said. "What a thing for Dr. Thompson to do! The idea! Is the man mad?"

"I told you, Joe," Mother said. "They'll take everything if we don't get away from here soon."

I heard the despair in her voice, and I saw it in her care-worn face.

"We owe Dr. Thompson about a thousand dollars. I didn't tell you, because I didn't want it to spoil our trip, but he sent a demand letter. I suppose this is his way of saying, 'Pay up, or else.'"

She stared at the empty space in the parlor where the organ should have been. "Oh, my beautiful organ! I bought it with my first teaching money when I was a girl!" Mother slumped into a chair and wept.

We had just returned from Yellowstone Park. Mother and Father had surprised us with the camping trip, knowing we would likely never come this far west again. For one whole week, Father pitched our tent wherever the day's end brought us. We slept hard, and in the mornings, washed in streams where thin sheets of ice shattered musically at the margins. Roaring waterfalls, Old Faithful, grizzly bears, everything seemed there for our particular pleasure. We enjoyed each other and the world around us, joking when small things went wrong, finding no need for harsh words, and for once, Father didn't worry about the weather. Never had I known such happy, care-free days.

The coolness of the house felt pleasant after so many days spent outdoors, yet already I longed for the smell of the pines, the cool breezes of the mountain valley, and the freedom from all these worries. We had been home only a few minutes, and already, trouble was beating us down.

Mother blew her nose and wiped her tears. "Joe, we'll have to move over the cook stove from the old house. I have to have something to cook on."

Eric stood at the door, twirling his hat, reluctant to go. "Pa was real upset. We all were. He said not to worry too much. Soon as you pay the bill, you'll get the things back, he's sure. He got his grain check and said the price is good, and yours will be too, he's sure. He wanted me to tell you that." He shuffled his boots on the stoop. "We're still hoping you won't move away, Mrs. O'Neill." His tone bordered on pleading.

"I don't know, Eric," said Mother. "It's pretty bad for us. We do thank you for your help. We'll pay you just as soon as the grain check comes."

Mother's steadfast refusal to entertain hope snuffed it out in me. Eric and I looked sadly at each other and said good-bye.

Father and Mother went to Edgemont the next morning.

"We went to the bank and signed over all our land, the buildings, the cattle, the horses, the pigs and chickens, the machinery, the harnesses, the saddle—everything but the household goods and the car," Father said.

"It won't pay all the mortgage, but almost all, and we threatened to file bankruptcy unless they accepted what we had," Mother said. "After the sale, we will be free of the bank."

"The O'Neill place will be no more," Father said. He sounded relieved, but the pain in his eyes said otherwise. "We tried to talk to Dr. Thompson, but he's out of town. Good thing he is. I was ready to tell him what I thought of him, and I'm wondering if I could have acted like a Christian."

"I'll write him another letter," Mother said. "He knows we'll pay him just as soon as we can. That man!"

The next day, we heard the Howells had been foreclosed on, and that Dr. Thompson had put a lien on their furniture—even their dishes.

"Do you suppose he would do that to us?" Mother fretted. "Oh, Joe. Can't we go right away and let Mr. Cass handle the sale?"

Four days later, in the gray dawn, Verna and I helped Mother pack up the Ford sedan. In less than an hour, Mother, we children, and Eric Cass would drive away, leaving Father to handle the sale. Eric, who was going to college not far from DeSmet in Brookings, had volunteered to help Mother with the driving.

Tom Cole had already pulled away with all our household possessions in a borrowed truck. He'd insisted on staying with us even after Father and Mother assured him that we must leave the homestead.

"I'll help you move," he'd said. "You're the nearest to folks I've had for awhile. Why shouldn't I be with you, if I can help?" It was the nearest he ever came to telling us anything about his life.

I wandered through the empty rooms one last time. The little cook stove, a bed, a chair, a table, and a few dishes were all we'd left behind for Father. The elegant porcelain bathtub that we'd never used, because there was no running water, stood gleaming in our modern bathroom. I think Mother would have taken it along if there'd been room.

I thought of how unbearably happy I'd been in our beautiful new house on my thirteenth birthday. My friends and I had gathered around the piano in this parlor, empty now, but full of echoes.

I gazed out the window at the little cedar tree and felt the cool air again of that spring morning Father and I had brought it home. Tears welled up, as I recalled how carefully we had transplanted it and how faithfully I had watered it through the heat and drought. Father had said, "If the tree is strong enough, the transplanting won't harm it." Now that it was my turn to be transplanted, I didn't feel strong or brave at all.

I slipped out the front door and dashed to the barn. Duke stood in the cool stall and turned his head to look at me. I paused in the doorway, letting my eyes adjust to the dark. My beautiful, wise Duke—so fleet-footed, so gentle, so enduring. He was more than a horse. He was my companion, my guardian. I felt safe from everything on his back. He warned me if there was a snake. He sensed the bolting of a steer from the herd and headed it off before it got started. He was sure-footed and wise about sliding shale and slippery grass. He had never failed me. I pressed my face against his neck and wound my hands in his black mane and wept.

"Lenna, Lenna, don't cry." Father's voice sounded as sorrowful as I felt. "It's hard, but it has to be. We're in God's hands. I've prayed about it and feel sure this is right for us all. The transplanting is difficult, but there's happiness ahead. We must be brave for each other's sake."

I rubbed the tears away with my fists. "It's so hard to leave, Papa!"

"I know. Come on, my girl. Mama is almost ready, and Eric and his father are here. Be brave. I love you very much." He held me close and led me out of the barn.

Out in the yard, Fanny pushed her cool nose into my hand, sneezed, and shook her head. Father had said he might bring her with him, but he hadn't promised.

"I think if I can find a good home for her, she would be happier here. She's not a house dog. She's a cattle dog," he'd said.

She was impatient with me, disappointed because she had expected that I would saddle Duke and we would be off somewhere together. I stooped and stroked her head, then ran into the house. I tried to hide my tears as I helped Eric carry out the last few things Mother deposited in our arms.

Mr. Cass teased me, trying to cheer me. "So, you're running away with my oldest son. Fine thing. Now you take good care of my cowboy." He was always saying embarrassing things like that. I knew, though, that he was sad too. After all, his boy was going away with us.

At last we were all in the car—all except Mother.

"Take care of yourself, Joe," she said and threw her arms about him and kissed him. She turned to Mr. Cass and shook his hand. "Thank you, Fred, for all you've done for us through the years. You helped us come here, and now you are watching us leave. We're proud to have known you and never will forget you."

She kissed Father again and took one last look around before she got in the car. My throat burned from holding back the tears. Father smiled bravely. Standing in the middle of the yard, he looked thin and small and so alone.

The little cedar by the front gate bowed in the wind as we swept by and headed down the lane.

About the Author

When her family homesteaded in 1915, seven-year-old Lenna O'Neill found her first love: the South Dakota prairie. Born in Wisconsin where her Irish immigrant father had come to study for the ministry, she discovered best friends in her pony Duke and her collie Fanny as she adapted to the harshness of prairie life. Eventually the hard times of drought and the depressed economy drove the family back to live in a town, but she never forgot the wonders of her life as a child on the South Dakota prairie.

Through the lens of time and distance, Lenna recorded her life during these prairie years for her family. *Child of the South Dakota Frontier* is an edited version of her recollections, published as a tribute by her daughter, BJ Farmer. Lenna opens her account with a return to the homestead years later with her husband, William Kolash, and her children. The lone tree remaining by a dilapidated front gate, planted by Lenna and her father decades before, recalls voices echoing from the past and memories that rolled away the years.